POPCORN SUTTON
THE MAKING AND MARKETING OF A HILLBILLY HERO

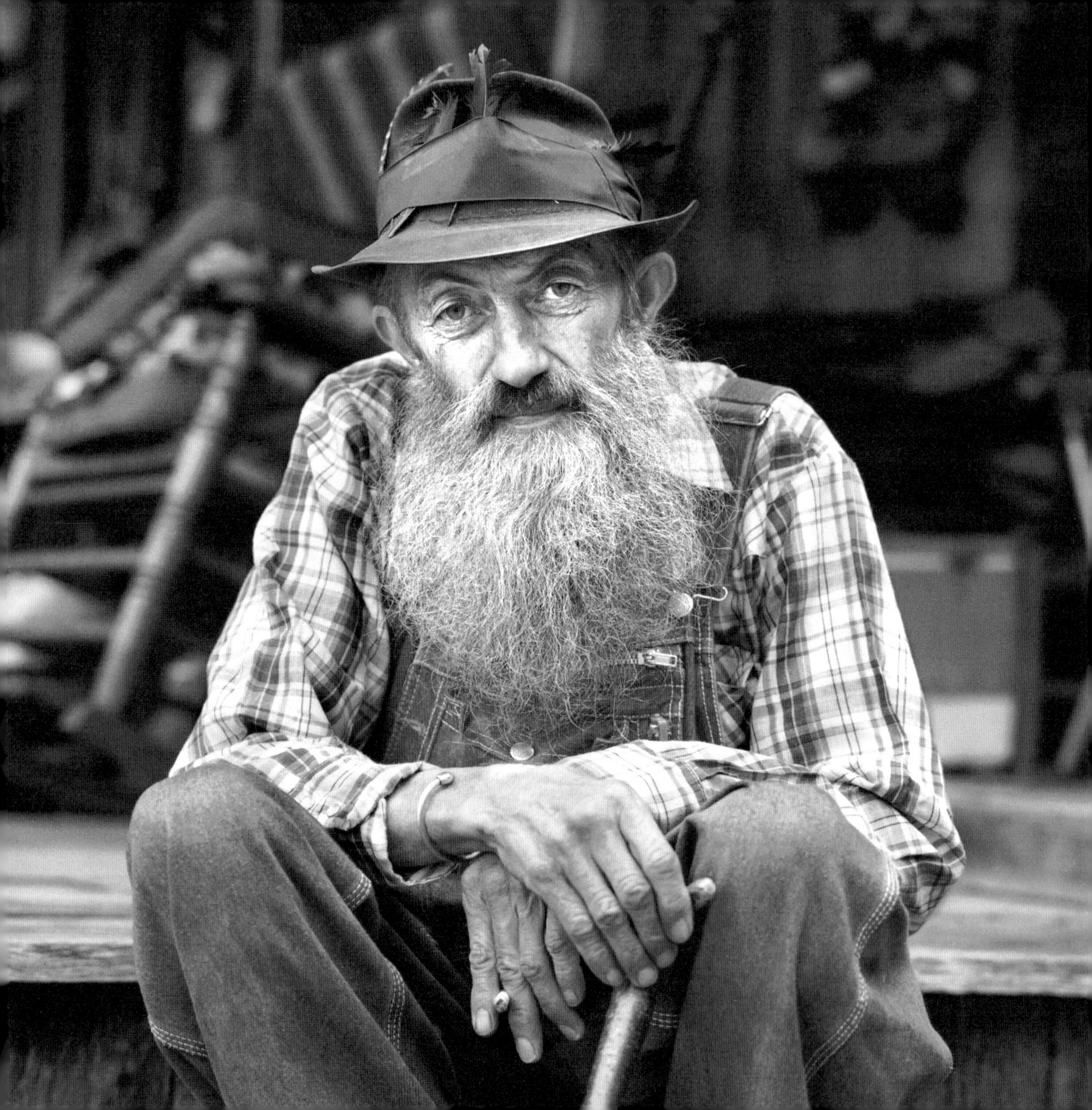

POPCORN SUTTON

THE MAKING AND MARKETING OF A HILLBILLY HERO

Text by Tom Wilson Jester • Photographs by Don Dudenbostel

Popcorn Sutton
The Making and Marketing of a Hillbilly Hero

Book design and composition by Cynthia Tollefsrud

Printed in the United States of America

ISBN 978-0-615-58513-0

DEDICATED TO POPCORN SUTTON

1947-2009

So long, Popcorn. Ain't gonna be no more like you.

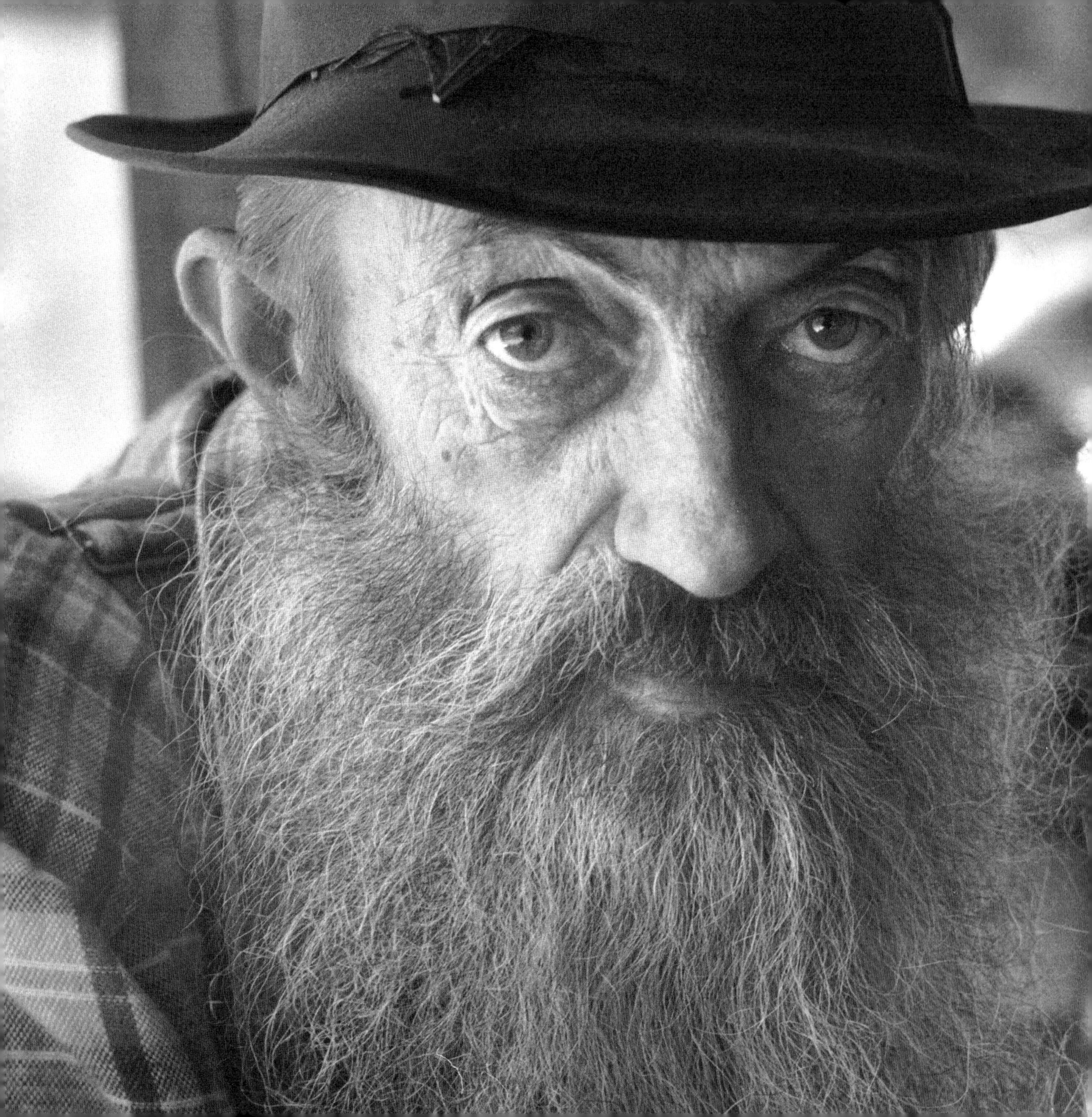

INTRODUCTION

EVERYBODY from around here in East Tennessee knows all about Popcorn Sutton, probably the most famous Appalachian moonshiner of all time.

Here's most of what everybody really knows about Popcorn Sutton:

Popcorn was a character, a true mountain man, a notorious moonshiner, a vile, foul-mouthed diminutive career criminal who didn't give a damn about the law. Everybody around here also knows that when Popcorn was busted for the last time, convicted of moonshining, violation of probation, possession of a firearm by a convicted felon and sentenced to a stretch in federal prison, he killed himself three days before he was to begin serving his sentence. That's all true. But it's also true Marvin Sutton was a real human being who had a different side to him than the one everybody claims to know.

Photographer Don Dudenbostel and I met with Popcorn extensively over a three-year period so Don could make black and white photographs while I made field recordings. Don shoots with relatively low-tech film; I use a relatively high-tech digital recorder and shotgun microphone. We did this as part of a continuing project to document the old Appalachia that is rapidly fading to black as times change and the old ways are left behind. We got to know Popcorn well during that time as we gradually got past the many firewalls, shields, force fields and layers of character that insulated his core and kept him famous and in business.

Popcorn was complicated. He wasn't just a hillbilly cartoon, the kind you see portrayed so much in touristy Appalachia restaurants advertising "kuntry cookin" with "aigs" for breakfast.

Popcorn Sutton was a cultural icon in a region where scofflaws are folk heroes and have been from way back. It's a tradition that goes all the way back to Scottish Highlands and Irish Protestants. He was not the kind of man with which most people outside the Appalachian mountains would want to get acquainted. Except for people with a taste for probably narcissistic, sociopathic criminals with a definite violent streak. But in the sometimes lawless Appalachians, that kind of personality can take you pretty far if you play it just right. And Popcorn did.

He understood he could never play the "Popcorn Sutton" role anywhere in the world except center stage in the heart of old Appalachia. "Up north," he'd be just another incorrigible criminal with a name well known to police. Out west, he'd be just another outlaw. But in the mountains of East Tennessee and Western North Carolina, he was revered and supported financially for being a notorious hillbilly moonshiner.

He loved it.

Moonshine and the people who make it have been part of this culture for a long time, at least since the Whisky Rebellion, or Whisky Insurrection, in the middle 1790s. This was President Washington's idea of a good way to pay for the American Revolution. Bad idea, it turned out, but it sure gave moonshining a boost as a business category.

So, since moonshining and those who make it have become so entrenched in the Appalachian mountain culture, characters like Popcorn (if, in fact, there ever was anybody exactly like Popcorn) have become part of the culture. Almost necessary icons confirming the truth at the core of our favorite stereotypes. It may not be much of an identity, but at least it's some kind of cultural identity. Every culture needs one.

Popcorn knew that better than anybody, and he worked it to perfection. But behind that hillbilly moonshiner stereotype, there's a lot more to Popcorn Sutton than you know, or maybe want to know.

This is the story of the Popcorn Sutton you don't know.

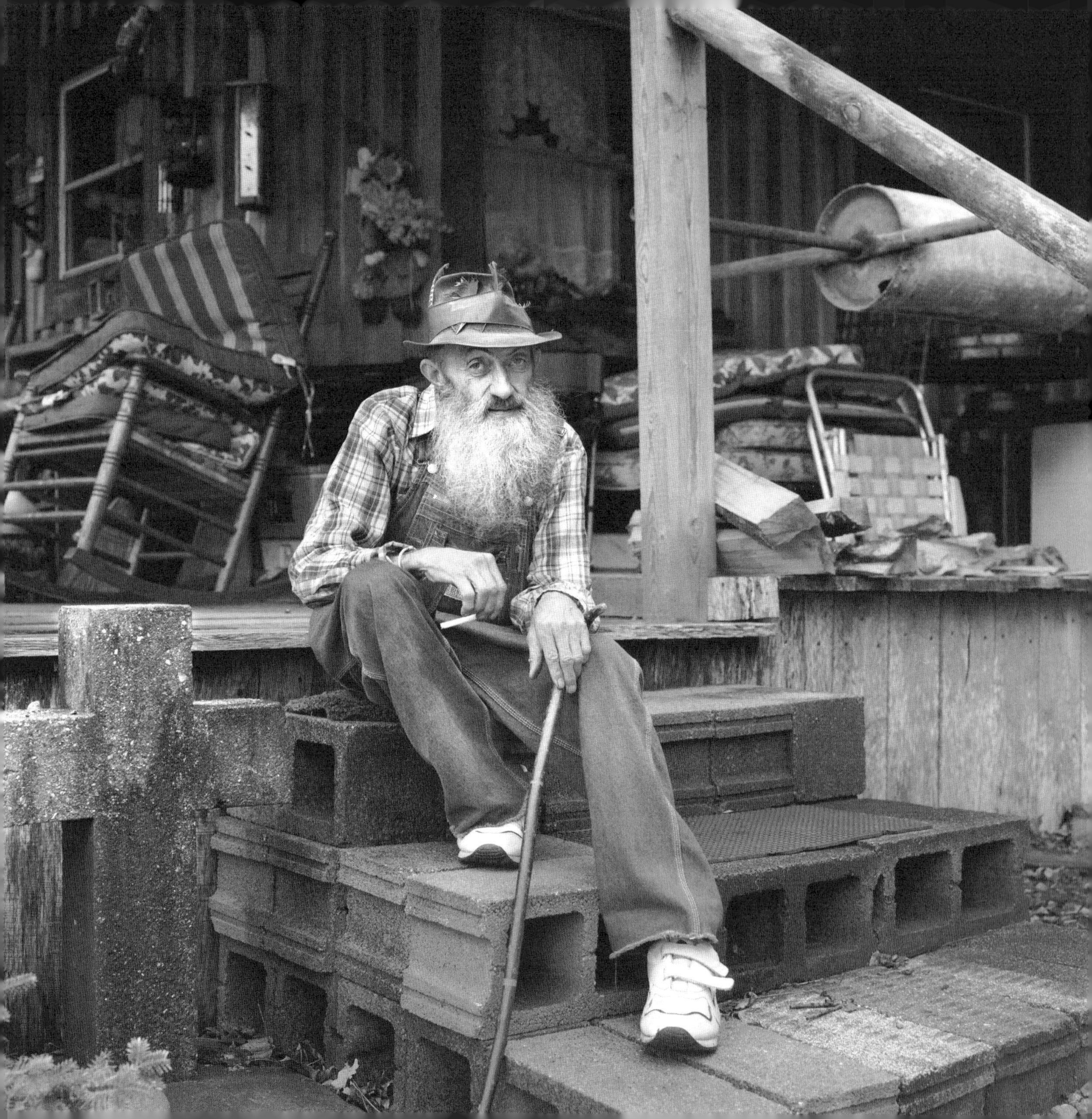

"Jesus turned the water into wine; I turned it into damn likker. And I don't think there's nothin' wrong with it, 'cause they drunk wine back in Biblical times and any kind of shit like that, beer, wine, alky-hol, homebrew, it'll all make ye drunk, so I figger alky-hol is alky-hol."

- Popcorn Sutton

THE LOOK WAS JUST too perfect not to be yet another hillbilly cartoon; everything was there except the corncob pipe stuck through the conical "hillbilly hat" they sell to tourists in vacation towns "nestled in the Smokies."

Popcorn looked like a page straight out of the hillbilly moonshiner stereotype playbook. The overalls, the long unkempt beard, the thick Appalachian mountain dialect, the foul talk, the back country outlaw's bravado.

Don Dudenbostel and I were working on a project for the East Tennessee History Center in Knoxville. We called the project *Vanishing Appalachia* and it was to be the result of a lifetime of documentary photography Don had done, plus three years of field interviews I recorded. Moonshining's certainly a part of old Appalachia, at least moonshining the old-fashioned way, and nobody was better known for that than one Marvin "Popcorn" Sutton. I'd seen him before on a cable channel show about moonshine, and Don had found out about him by just asking around. It's interesting – and telling – how Don got Popcorn's cell phone number.

He called Maggie Valley information.

"A friend of mine told me about Popcorn Sutton," Don remembers. "He described him as a 'crazy moonshiner' over in North Carolina on the Smokies side. This Popcorn character sounded pretty interesting, but I couldn't find anybody who knew how to get in touch with him. I found out he lived in Maggie Valley, so I called up the information operator and she gave me Popcorn's cell phone number. Everybody knew him.

"I called him up and started discussing what we wanted to do and Popcorn went into the 'I'm a dying man' routine, which we heard many times after that. I told him I'd be happy to call him back if he wasn't up to it. But Popcorn liked the spotlight and was a real publicity hound so we set up a time to meet."

Don called the cell phone, which Popcorn kept in the bib of his overalls. The cell phone in the overalls was the first clue that we were about to meet a living anachronism. Maggie Valley is a little tourist town in Haywood County, N.C., just over the Tennessee state line. It's another one that advertises itself as being "nestled in the Smokies." Popcorn arranged to meet Don behind a little theatre playhouse.

THE HAT. THE CIGARETTE. THE OVERALLS.

POPCORN'S hillbilly stereotype was so well-drawn and so obviously commercialized, I had to wonder when I first met him: "Is this guy real?"

I'd seen him before on a cable TV network show about moonshiners, but this was my first look at him in person. He had the long scruffy grey beard, wore faded Liberty bib overalls and a greasy old fedora. The hat was decorated with a squirrel's tail and feathers stuck in the headband and a peculiarly shaped bone piercing the point of the hat's crown. When I

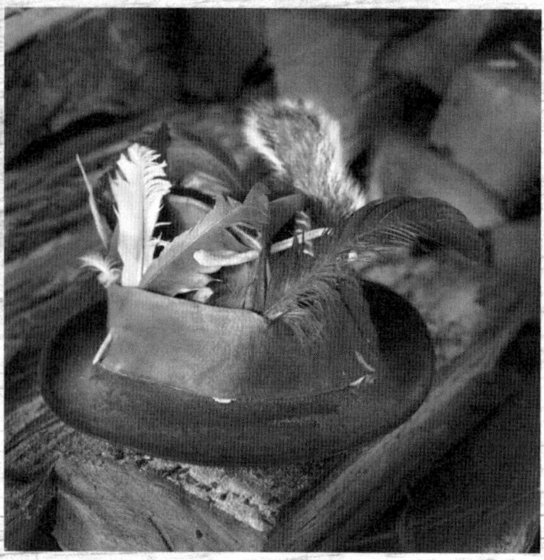

asked him what that was, he described it matter-of-factly as, "a coon peter" which is a vernacular term for a raccoon penis bone. Popcorn explained that old-timers used them as toothpicks, but he used the one in his hat for cleaning out burner hoses and nozzles in his still. He had it stuck in the point of the hat's crown to keep it always handy during a moonshine run.

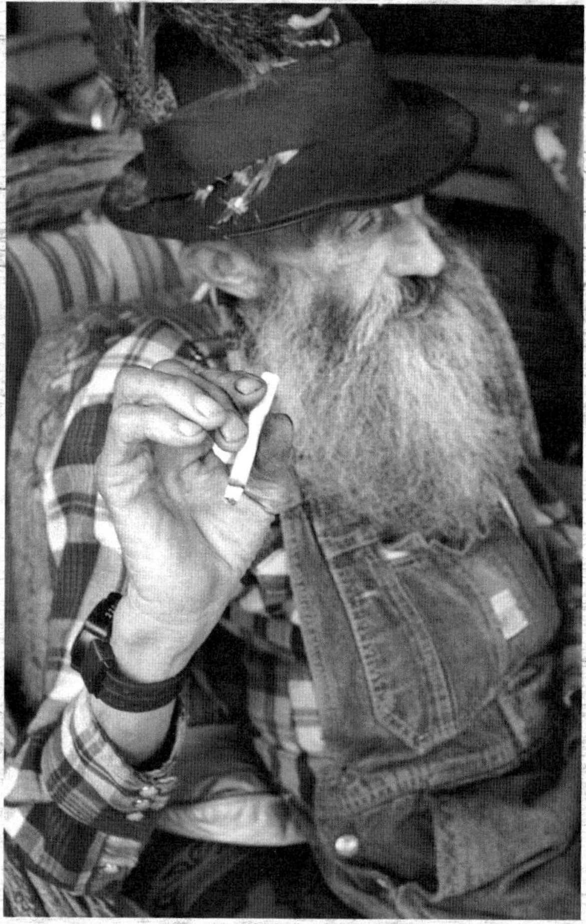

Popcorn smoked constantly between coughs, lighting one unfiltered cigarette off the other from the time he got up in the morning until he went to bed at night. One of Popcorn's standard lines about his smoking was that "I get more use outta one of them Bic lighters than anybody else in the world. I just use it onest a day to light the first 'un." He also liked to say he smoked only unfiltered cigarettes "because I don't like smokin' through a muffler."

"I been smokin' since I was six years old and I ain't quit yet. Somethin's gonna gitchee, mize well be cig-rettes," was another of his standard comments about his smoking.

Hard to imagine Popcorn without his ever present, always lit cigarette, or the hat or the overalls.

After Popcorn died, I asked his widow to tell me something about Popcorn that nobody knew. She told me Popcorn had a secret reason for wearing the overalls. She said, "if you ever saw him without those overalls on, you'd see why." She said that Popcorn, short as he was, was oddly proportioned, and got most of whatever height he had from his legs. "He had a little ol' short body, and was mostly legs," she said. "He wore baggy overalls so you couldn't tell it."

The hat, the overalls, the cigarettes. Every good outlaw by tradition needs

good trademarks. But trademarks aren't enough. You also need a good nickname. And Marvin Sutton got himself a real good one. Marvin Sutton became Popcorn Sutton after one night spent at a tavern when he was in his 20s and "three-thirds drunk." The thoroughly drunk Marvin Sutton put a dime in a popcorn machine and the machine yielded no popcorn. So thoroughly drunk and now enraged, Marvin Sutton took up a pool cue and smashed the offending machine to pieces.

When Marvin went back to that tavern the next day to pay the owner for the busted popcorn machine ($75), a guy at the bar who'd been there the night before recognized him and said, "Well, here comes ol' Popcorn!" Getting such a marketable and permanent nickname turned out to be the best $75 Marvin "Popcorn" Sutton ever spent.

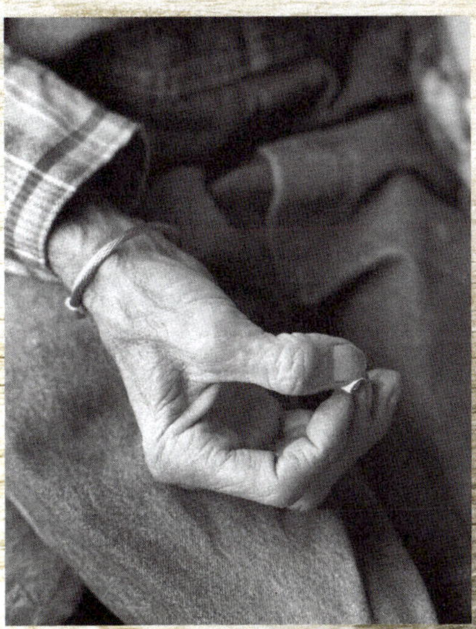

In tourist season, Popcorn himself was one of the attractions. For a fee, you could have your picture made with Popcorn Sutton, a real mountain man moonshiner posing by a still he constructed on the back of a restored Model A Ford pick-up. He sold autographed pictures of himself and sold the "hillbilly hats" required by tourist trade. He also ran an "antique store" in Maggie Valley and, oh yeah, sold moonshine using the "store" as a front. No big secret about that; everybody knew about it.

The old moonshiner was big business in Maggie Valley, and brought in a lot of tourist dollars to this tourist town, so everyone there, from the information operator to the chamber of commerce, was only too happy to help. The law cooperated, too, by not paying too much attention to Popcorn's selling his illegal moonshine using an antique store as a front – wink, wink.

Don took his wife, Cynthia, along with him to meet the notorious Popcorn. That turned out to be a big mistake -- more about that later. Don and Cynthia were waiting for Popcorn in the gravel parking lot behind the playhouse when Popcorn came careening in, "driving a little pick-up truck at about 70 miles an hour and throwing gravel everywhere."

At that first meeting, Popcorn gave Don what turned out to be his standard spiel about the glories and hazards of being a moonshiner. Apparently to impress upon Don about what a true outlaw he was, Popcorn told the story about how his sister had tried to burn his house down with everybody in it and turn him in to the law. He swore he'd kill her and her husband if he ever saw them again, then produced a loaded small caliber revolver from the bib of his overalls, where he also kept his cell phone. His cell phone was loaded, too, but with the names of customers on speed dial.

"No question this guy was a stereotype, but definitely a real person, more than just a front. Some of it was, but that was just his lifestyle," Don said.

"Popcorn did a lot of talking that first meeting about cutting throats and shooting people," Don said, "and I think he meant it. Popcorn really was a violent person, I found out later." That was also the first time Don asked himself the question, "what have I gotten myself into this time?" I asked Don a variation of this question a lot as we got to know Popcorn.

After the warm-up talk about cutting some people's throats and shooting others, Popcorn began a stream of ramblings about women in a very crude way. That was the moment Don realized bringing Cynthia to meet Popcorn was probably a mistake. Don's wife is a well-known and successful painter.

"I wouldn't have a damn old skinny-aise woman. I'd just kick her outta bed. I'm cold natured and I have to have a woman with a big aise to keep me warm in my cabin durin' the winter."

Popcorn Sutton

She's also a Lutheran minister's daughter from Minnesota, but even so, she's no prude.

Still, Cynthia could take only so much of Popcorn's talk before she started getting a serious case of the creeps. Especially when Popcorn started describing in detail various parts of his anatomy and how he used them with women.

Popcorn was maybe five and a half feet tall, maybe a little taller, but he was a small man who liked big women. Women, he said, "with an aise as big as a tractor tire."

"I wouldn't have a damn old skinny-aise woman," he said," I'd just kick her outta bed. I'm cold natured and I have to have a woman with a big aise to keep me warm in my cabin durin' the winter."

NOW, ABOUT THIS TERM "HILLBILLY"

THEY MAY TRADE on the term here in the mountains, but if you want to find out what they really think of it, try referring to someone that way here in the mountains.

Especially if you're "from off summers" (off somewhere, not from around here). You probably won't like what happens next. Appalachian mountain people are proud folk, descended from a long line of proud folk who've survived tough times for centuries. In fact, the term "hillbilly" refers to a derogatory term used by the English and Irish Catholics to refer to Protestants from the hilly Irish countryside who were loyal to the Protestant king of Ireland. That king was William of Orange, a relative of English royalty imported from the Netherlands to rule Ireland and make it Protestant.

As hatred for William of Orange grew, his name became all the more diminutive to reflect lack of respect. So William became Billy. People from the hills of Northern Ireland who were Protestant supporters of King Billy

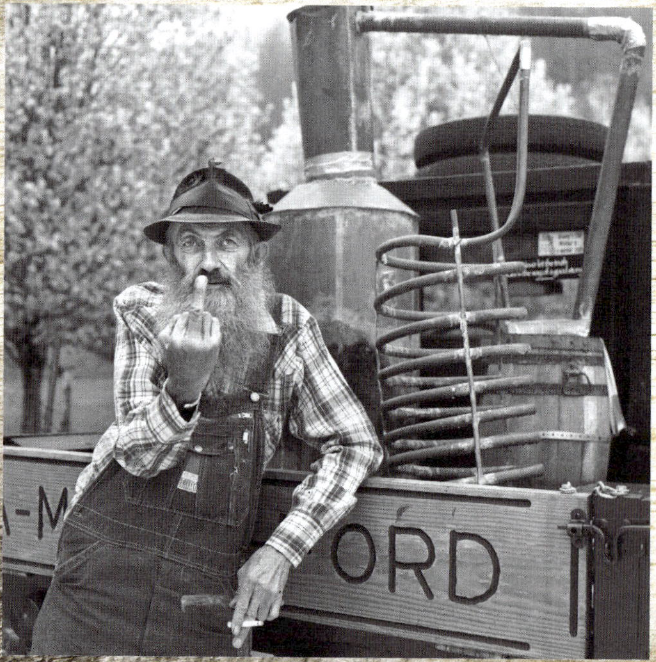

became referred to, most disparagingly, as inelegant "hillbillies."

The Protestant Scots-Irish weren't given much of a choice by the English back in the 1600s and early 1700s. They were told to prosper the land or get out. Then, as now, Scots-Irish mountain people have a genetic hatred for aristocracy and don't take kindly to being told by them what to do. So they left the Protestant settlements of Northern Ireland, the lowlands and border lands of Scotland, packed up their attitudes along with their possessions and took them both to America.

Their descendants among the Appalachian highlanders are used to hardship from way back. And no matter what, they mean to stay with their land and they'll fight anybody who says they can't.

That's the stock Popcorn came from.

The real difference between hillbillies and the rest of us is poverty and lack of education, two dark forms overlaying the mountains, like shadows at sundown .

Sure, they can be guarded and suspicious of strangers, maybe even hostile to the point of firearms, but they can also be the most open, generous, warm hearted and giving people you could ever hope to meet. The poorest have nothing, not even dreams. But because they truly know what it means to be a loser in the war on poverty, they'll be the first to give you what they do have if you need it.

That is, if they know you. If they don't know you, they won't give you directions to the post office. In these mountains, as it has been for two centuries, survival is everything. You do what you have to do toward that end, beginning with cultivating a healthy distrust of outsiders. When outsiders came into Appalachia they plundered the abundant natural resources from Pennsylvania to West Virginia to Tennessee – coal, timber and cheap labor. It's a story that hasn't had a good outcome for the mountain people themselves. The outsider business pirates took home the money and resources from Appalachia, leaving the mountain people little more than their pride.

So, Popcorn, like many here, figured that if he had to play to the stereotype, he might as well make some money on it and maybe take some money back from the "outlanders."

The late "Chief Henry," whose real name was Henry Lambert, did exactly that in Cherokee, N.C., until he retired in 1985 after "chiefin'" for 50 years. Posing in front of a sheet metal teepee and wearing an elaborately feathered war bonnet, the kind kids of the time would recognize from movie westerns, Chief Henry was a hundred years and half a country away from the Plains Indians whose costume he'd adopted for the station wagon tourist trade.

"The World's Most Photographed Indian" died in 2007, maintaining to the end of his life he was proud of what he did.

Nowadays, playing to the stereotype has mostly disappeared as a way for a real Cherokee to make a living in his or her namesake town. The sheet metal teepee and bear pits have been supplanted by Harrah's Casino. Not one of the noble and storied Cherokee's finest moments, but it's a living.

From Popcorn Sutton to Chief Henry to Col. Sanders, the stereotypical representation is a "brandable image" (to use the marketing buzzword) and there's money to be made with it.

Knowing the real history of the proud Cherokee people, including the forced march removal known as "The Trail of Tears," you know "chiefin'" had to be conflicting for Henry Lambert, at least on a genetic level. And if you know anything about Old South plantations and the gentry who owned both the land and the enslaved people who worked it, Col. Sanders is just embarrassing. Not at all "finger-lickin' good" – whatever that means.

Popcorn honestly loved moonshining and all the attention and the notoriety that came with it, but he was a proud man, and playing to the hillbilly stereotype is really nothing to be proud of. Especially for a real hillbilly.

Still, there's always some truth behind stereotypes – they have to come from somewhere.

RELIGION AND ALCOHOL

IN THIS CULTURE, religion and moonshine are intertwined. Drinking moonshine and church going (but not at the same time) are staples of old Appalachian culture. Both these activities don't define the culture; they're just a part of the bigger picture, along with quilting and growing pole beans. Drinking moonshine is one thing people here who don't have a lot of options do when they need to feel better, and "hit don't cost a lot."

It's also a carryover from the region's early settlers, the immigrants from the Scottish Lowlands and Northern Ireland. According to Jim Webb, author of *Born Fighting: How the Scots-Irish Shaped America*, these were people for whom "drinking and praying go hand-in-hand with fighting and singing."

"Hell no, goddammit. If it's Sunday I'll be in church."

Popcorn Sutton

Popcorn left the parking lot the same way he came in, gunning his pick-up and spraying gravel everywhere.

Cynthia said she couldn't wait to get home to take a long shower. A very long shower.

Don never again brought her anywhere near Popcorn Sutton.

If you got to know Popcorn you eventually realized his talk about women and references to certain parts of his anatomy were part of his standard routine. He used that on everybody, especially when there were women present, just to see what would happen. People who knew Popcorn explained this as, "Aw, 'at's just Popcorn bein' Popcorn." Yes, Popcorn being Popcorn to get attention for himself and to make sure you understood he was a real mountain man outlaw. In the mountains of Appalachia, if "you're not from around here," or don't have the same name as those on a lot of local tombstones, you don't always get a big display hospitality anyway. Down and dirty cussing is just part of the Appalachian *lingua franca* and everybody does it except bankers and preachers.

Popcorn really liked to cuss, though, and would go to some trouble to work a cussword into a sentence even when it didn't make any sense. "Overalls is all I ever damn wear," he said to me once.

Popcorn was as fond of making religious references as he was of cussing, often saying how he prayed on his knees every night and went to church at every opportunity.

One time Don asked Popcorn if he could come up to his cabin one Sunday for a photo session. This gave Popcorn a unique opportunity to both cuss and make a statement about how religious he was at the same time. "Hell no, goddammit," Popcorn answered, "If it's Sunday I'll be in church."

So, soon after Don's first meeting with Popcorn in the summer of 2007, Don and I were off to Maggie Valley to meet Popcorn at the Misty Mountain Ranch Bed and Breakfast in Maggie Valley. It was Don's second meeting with Popcorn and my first. He made photographs and, after Don finished his shoot, I recorded an interview. Popcorn was a natural photo subject, by the way, switching from pose to pose effortlessly and never missing a chance to engage the camera. "The camera loves him," they would have said in Hollywood.

On that first day of interviewing Popcorn, I had a lot to think about as we talked about the moonshiner's life and how much work it was. "It's the hardest work you'll ever do," he told me. Popcorn took Don and me up to a cabin near there where he lived when he was in Maggie Valley. It was there on the porch steps in front of that cabin where Don made the now famous portrait shot of Popcorn.

That day at the cabin in "Maggie" was the first time I saw Popcorn's "Three Jar Ford." That was an old Ford car, I think 70's vintage, that Popcorn got in trade, as the name implies, for three jars of moonshine. Jars refers to the clear "Mason jars" used both for "puttin' up" (canning) garden vegetables and for moonshine. When Popcorn referred to a "jar a'likker" he meant a quart jar.

Popcorn had spray painted the car "John Deere green," affixed "a "Three Jar Ford" decal to the rear window and souped up the engine. He took the car on a long trip out West, then hardly used it again for the next three years.

After Don and I concluded our photo/interview session, I bought a half-gallon jug of Popcorn's finest for a friend of mine and Popcorn tried to turn Don into a distributor. Popcorn, no slouch at business, presented Don with carefully worked out financial arrangements he'd figured down to the penny. Don politely declined, saying he'd rather stake his career on photography instead of moonshining and he'd like to stay married.

MISTY MOUNTAIN RANCH B&B

OWNERS KAREN HESSION and her husband were old friends with Popcorn, and even had a dedicated "Popcorn Sutton" suite at their bed and breakfast. Today, on the Misty Mountain Ranch website, they use a cartoon version of Popcorn as part of their logo and you can still make a reservation for a stay in the Popcorn Sutton suite.

The cartoon isn't much of a true likeness; it bears only passing resemblance to Popcorn. The character is also drawn with a classic earthenware moonshine jug that has "Popcorn Sutton" written on it (instead of the usual XXX) just to make sure you get the point. Just to make really sure you get the point, the cartoon Popcorn also wears something like the real Popcorn's trademark hat with the feathers stuck in the hatband. There's also a slideshow on the website with a picture of the real Popcorn posing outside a room at the B&B.

Even after his death, Popcorn Sutton is still marketing gold for the tourist trade in Maggie Valley.

To be fair, Karen and Peter Hession really were long-time friends of Popcorn and are still happy to share stories of Popcorn's kinder side with any who ask. Popcorn was happy if his friends could make some money using his likeness. "Hell, why not make money off this shit?" Popcorn told Don and me, "I do."

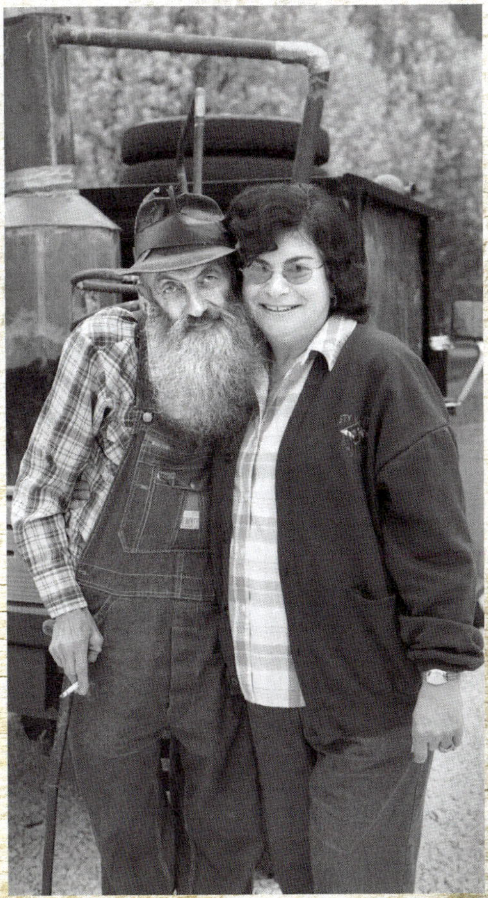

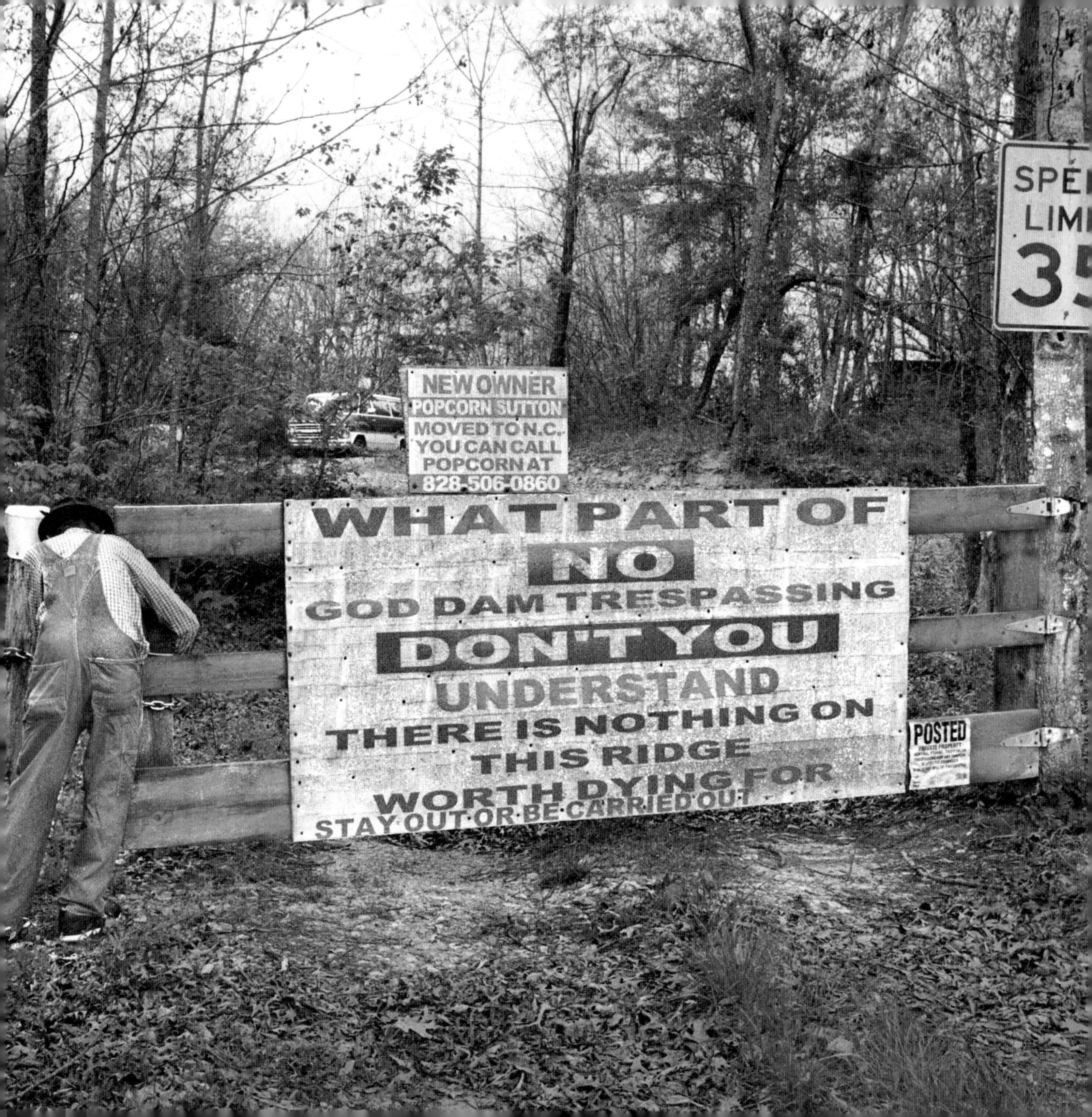
NEW OWNER
POPCORN SUTTON
MOVED TO N.C.
YOU CAN CALL
POPCORN AT
828-506-0860
WHAT PART OF
NO
GOD DAM TRESPASSING
DON'T YOU
UNDERSTAND
THERE IS NOTHING ON
THIS RIDGE
WORTH DYING FOR
STAY OUT OR BE CARRIED OUT
POSTED

"Ye ain't from around here, are ye?"

ONE DAY, DURING a photo/interview session with Popcorn in Maggie Valley, he said something to Don and me that really got our attention: "You come over to Parrottsville next week and I'm gonna show you something you've never seen before."

Boy, did he ever.

His instructions to us were to go to Parrottsville -- that's right outside of Newport in Cocke County and wait for him.

We did as Popcorn instructed us to do. We went in to the Country Cafe and got breakfast, the usual bacon-and-egg fare served to us by a durable, country-as-cornbread woman wearing camouflage pattern army fatigues and a NASCAR T-shirt. Her hair was colored truck stop blonde. Country cool from camo to coiffure. Don and I had finished our breakfast and were just killing time with cups of coffee waiting for Popcorn to show up when the camo pants NASCAR waitress came up to our table and said, "Ye ain't from around here, are ye?"

I told her jokingly that I'd lived in the South all my life and had never been asked that question. I said around here that's the question we ask Yankees when they look like they're lost. So she just rephrased the question and asked us more directly where we were from and what we were doing here.

I didn't think Don and I looked more suspicious than a couple of old grey-beard hippies, so I didn't seen any harm in telling her we were from Knoxville and we were here waiting on a friend.

"Wouldn't be a skinny-aise old moonshiner would it?"

Don and I looked at each other and said, in unison, "Popcorn!"

That answer satisfied her and we were still laughing about it when Popcorn came in. Turns out the woman he intended to marry, Pam, was a cook at the Country Cafe, and Popcorn had called her ahead of our arrival to tell the folks there to watch for us.

"Everybody looks out for Popcorn around here," the camo pants NASCAR waitress told us later.

We sat with Popcorn while he finished his bacon, eggs and grits. But we couldn't go to Popcorn's house and still just yet. We had to pass another test and prove a point.

He told us to stop in at a local convenience store and ask the owner there if he knew where Marvin "Popcorn" Sutton lived, saying his name like it would read on a wanted poster, "and you tell me what he says."

Don and I went into the store and got a couple of soft drinks. We hadn't agreed beforehand on who was going to ask the question. But since I was paying first, I decided to ask. I drew a breath to speak, but before I could get the words out, Don beat me to it. "Do you know where Marvin 'Popcorn' Sutton lives?"

The man at the register, the owner, suddenly forgot how to speak in complete sentences but managed to cobble together enough words to say something that sounded a lot like, "I've heard of him, but I don't think he lives around here. He mighta been in here before, but I don't know where he lives."

"Ah, Popcorn put us up to it," Don said.

The store owner, who Popcorn later told us was a Cocke County constable, said nothing. Satisfied that we had proved the point that "everybody looks out for Popcorn around here," Don and I left the store at a brisk walk, got in Don's car and drove to Popcorn's place just down the road a couple of miles.

The directions Popcorn gave us were through the back way, a gated and locked entrance a distance behind his house. There was a sign he'd made that covered most of the gate. It read:

WHAT PART OF
NO
GOD DAM TRESPASSING
DON'T YOU
UNDERSTAND.
THERE IS NOTHING ON
THIS RIDGE
WORTH DYING FOR
STAY OUT OR BE CARRIED OUT

Other signs on the gate included a standard "Posted" notice, the kind you can buy at the Farmer's Co-op, and one stating falsely that the property had a new owner, that Popcorn Sutton had moved to N.C. and you could call him at this number (his always-on cell phone, which was correct).

There was also another sign, this one not home made, that Popcorn had nailed to a tree on the right side of the gate:

SPEED
LIMIT
35

It was an official county speed limit sign that was undoubtedly stolen. Or maybe given to Popcorn by a constable.

BOOTLEGGER OR MOONSHINER?

ONE THING DON AND I learned right quick about Popcorn Sutton in the three years we knew him, both as a man and as a documentary subject, is that he was NOT a bootlegger. If you met him and called him that, it would be insulting enough that you'd get cussed out for sure, and maybe get a Case XX knife blade in your ribs to boot.

Bootlegger or moonshiner? There's a big difference.

A bootlegger sells legal alcohol illegally. Hell, anybody can sell whiskey out of a car or off a back porch on a Sunday. The "bootlegger" term comes from the practice hiding a bottle in the leg of a boot. The term "moonshining" comes from the practice of running stills at night, by the light of the moon, so the smoke from the wood-fired boiler could not be easily seen by the authorities.

Bootlegging is one story, but make no mistake, moonshining is another, and it's altogether different.

A moonshiner has a long tradition behind him of both making and selling, or at least distributing, illegal alcohol, usually corn whiskey, more commonly called (and spelled) "corn likker." Terms, like "white lightnin'," "corn squeezins" and "mountain dew," are well known, made popular by songs like *That Good Old Mountain Dew* and *White Lightnin'.* Nobody uses any of those names in old Appalachia.

Here, it's only "moonshine" or, usually, just "shine." Popcorn, who was as world-school as it gets, favored the term "likker" and spelled it that way in the title of his self-published book, *Me and My Likker.*

Moonshining's indisputably an Appalachian mountain tradition, no matter what you call it. And there's another long tradition that goes along with it. That's the other tradition that has shadowed moonshiners since the beginning. That's the government's tradition of "lawing" them. For a revenuer – that's a government man whose job it is to bust up stills and haul the operators off to jail -- it's better to nab a moonshiner than a bootlegger. Moonshiners take more income away from the state than bootleggers do, and the states pay the revenuer's salary. In this part of the world, the more illegal you are when it comes to distribution of alcohol, the more fame, or infamy, is attached to your name. And the more illegal, the better, as far as sales are concerned.

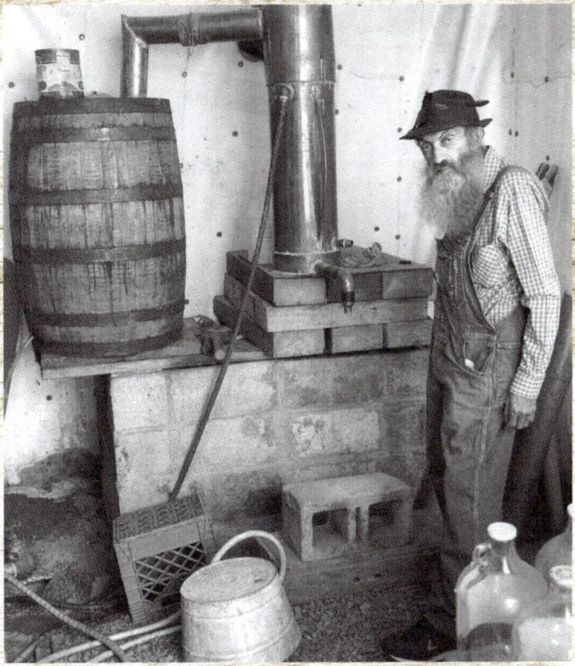

The revenuers have developed a grudging respect for their sworn enemies, the moonshiners, and the feeling's mutual.

In back country Appalachia bootlegging is illegal, but moonshining's only illegal if you get caught.

Even though Popcorn probably wouldn't know who Voltaire was and doubtless wouldn't care, he knew full well that if there were no Popcorn Sutton in these mountains, it would have been necessary to invent one.

So Marvin Sutton, third-generation moonshiner by trade, invented Popcorn Sutton and figured out how to market a version of himself that turned him into gen-u-wine hillbilly hero.

That was on Tuesday, April 24, 2007, the day Don and I were introduced to a real moonshining still operation.

Maybe a little too real, as it turned out.

Popcorn began our tour by taking us to a shed where he stored his supplies, including sacks of malt from Bamberg, Germany. Popcorn began loading malt from the bags into to an old coffee grinder he said was made in 1948. "Come outta an old A&P," he said. It was probably used to grind arabica beans for Eight O'Clock Coffee, the original A&P store brand.

With the grinder doing its work now for moonshine instead of coffee Popcorn began his spiel about the quality of his moonshine as if he were talking at a trade show. "This malt right here, in these bags, costs a dollar and fifty-two cents a pound. Now who in the hell is going to spend that kind of money? Nobody but me. Everybody else makes it outta wheat bran, what you call 'shorts.' They make it outta wheat bran, sugar, and put about ten bag of yeast in it. And that's all's in it. There's no malt flavor, no malt smell, no nothin'. Mine's made outta actually pure malt. Ain't no meal in it. If you're gonna make it, make it first class or get outta business."

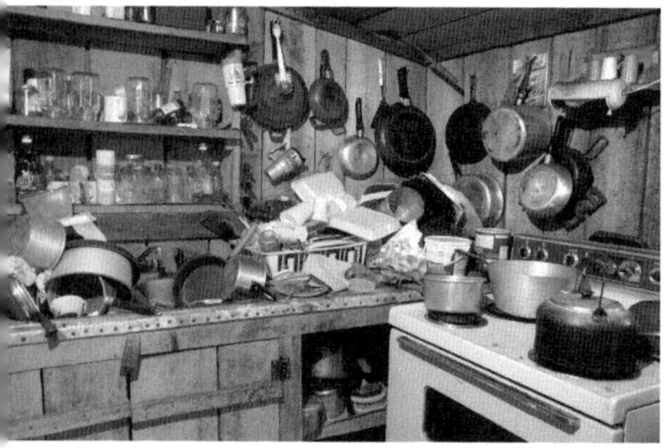

With the malt grinding done, Popcorn showed us the propane and gas tanks outside the still house that powered the burners for the big stills inside. He didn't show us the still just yet. Before we could see them, Popcorn wanted to show us around his property, beginning with a ramshackle little house in the woods he called his "nigger shack".

Once inside, he tried to sell me a "very valuable" stringless violin he said was made in Italy a long time ago. Just by tapping the wood you could hear it had the acoustics of an empty Prince Albert tobacco can, and was probably worth about the same. There was a label on the inside that looked like it came off a pack of firecrackers. The only thing on that label written in English said, "Made in Japan".

Popcorn always had some kind of con going. When we first met him at Maggie Valley, he wanted his picture made with a fine old Gibson 5-string banjo he'd gotten somewhere. It was a customized Gibson Mastertone, really worth something, unlike the "Italian" violin. Well, worth something to a serious banjo player, which Popcorn certainly was not. He couldn't play a note and just used the Mastertone as a prop for pictures that might enhance his image as a backwoods hillbilly. Since *Deliverance*, everybody knows that all genetically compromised folks from back in the hills play the banjo, don't they? Just look at any of Don's pictures of Popcorn with his banjo and notice the way he's holding it. Both hand positions are wrong for actual banjo playing.

Popcorn also had a business card he'd printed up that described the services he rendered as, among other things, a video producer. Popcorn had been in some *YouTube* videos and a cable channel documentary or two, but he didn't know any more about producing a video than he did playing the banjo. He kept insisting that Don and I were "making a video," when I was using only a digital audio recorder with a shotgun microphone and Don was shooting film with a still camera. Only audio, only stills. No video camera. Popcorn didn't seem to know the difference, but he liked being in videos and so we didn't argue.

The first indication Don and I got that this day was somehow going to be different came when Popcorn sat on the shack's old toilet and insisted Don take his picture. Don tried to decline, but Popcorn wouldn't take no for an answer, and now Don has an image of Popcorn Sutton, overalls, feathered hat and all, sitting on an old, probably non-working, toilet. “Just when you think you’ve done it all,” Don is thinking, as he clicks off a few images.

Next along the shack tour, Popcorn showed us where his secret stash of moonshine was hidden behind a false wall. This he said was his insurance in case something happened. I can’t say how many half-gallon jugs were behind that wall, since we couldn’t see them, but my guess was about a hundred, maybe more. The old boarded wall was perilously close to a wood stove used to heat the rickety house, maybe only four feet away. I thought it would’ve required an equal measure of faith and luck to light that wood stove without lighting the house along with it.

Finally, Popcorn took us to his recently finished cabin. The cabin was smallish, maybe only 1,200 square feet, but it had a generous wrap-around porch that held not only an assortment of chairs but firewood and a lot of old tools he’d collected. Popcorn said he hoped to sell some of those old tools at his store in Maggie Valley.

Next to the porch steps was a marble footstone Popcorn had ordered for eventual placement at the foot of his grave. The inscription was a message carved in stone addressed to all who might one day visit his final resting place:

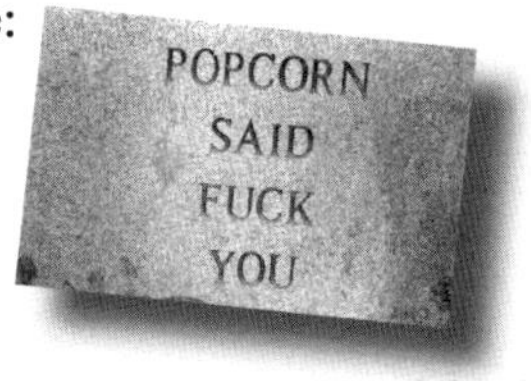

Inside, the place was surprisingly neat, considering all the stuff that was in there, a continuation of all the stuff that was on the porch. There were various bits of moonshining artifacts, including a couple of old copper coils. There were leg irons Popcorn said came from San Quentin prison. Old family photographs hung on the wall, some were hand colored and had antique oval frames. They hung next to some grisly old black and white police crime scene photographs. There was one small bedroom over to the left as you came in, which you had to notice because the ceiling was papered with hundreds of dollar bills, all lined up perfectly. Popcorn was actually a neat freak, and his house was always in spotless order, a condition known by people who look down on this kind of living as “country clean.”

And then there was that other room in the back -- the master bedroom -- where Popcorn kept a wooden coffin he’d bought at a good price for his eventual use. It had a raised Masonic emblem on it. Popcorn was no Mason, but the coffin had a nice dark finish and Popcorn got it cheap. He liked to pose for pictures lying in it, usually with his eyes rolled back and looking as dead as possible. He’s in that coffin now, but not to pose for pictures. He’s buried in it.

Did I mention that over the bed there’s an overhead mirror mounted on a slant to better reflect what’s going on beneath? And did I also mention that on either side of the mirror on the ceiling there are pulleys and ropes attached to a pair of oversized boots so the “operator” can raise and lower the legs of whoever’s feet are in those boots?

Well, I think I’ll just leave that one to your imagination, if you’ve got that kind of imagination. If you don’t, you don’t want to hear about it.

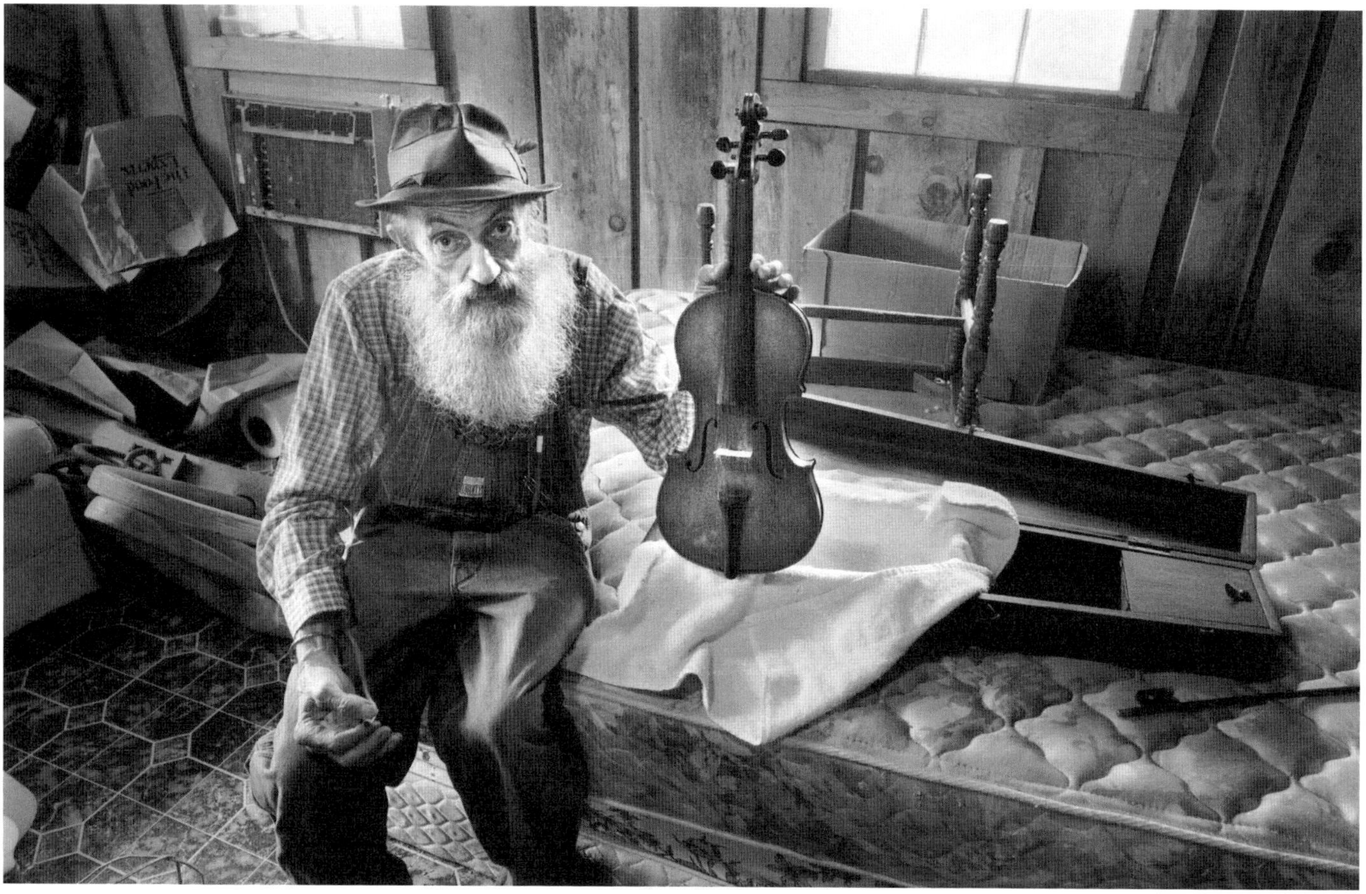

Popcorn's "Italian" Violin

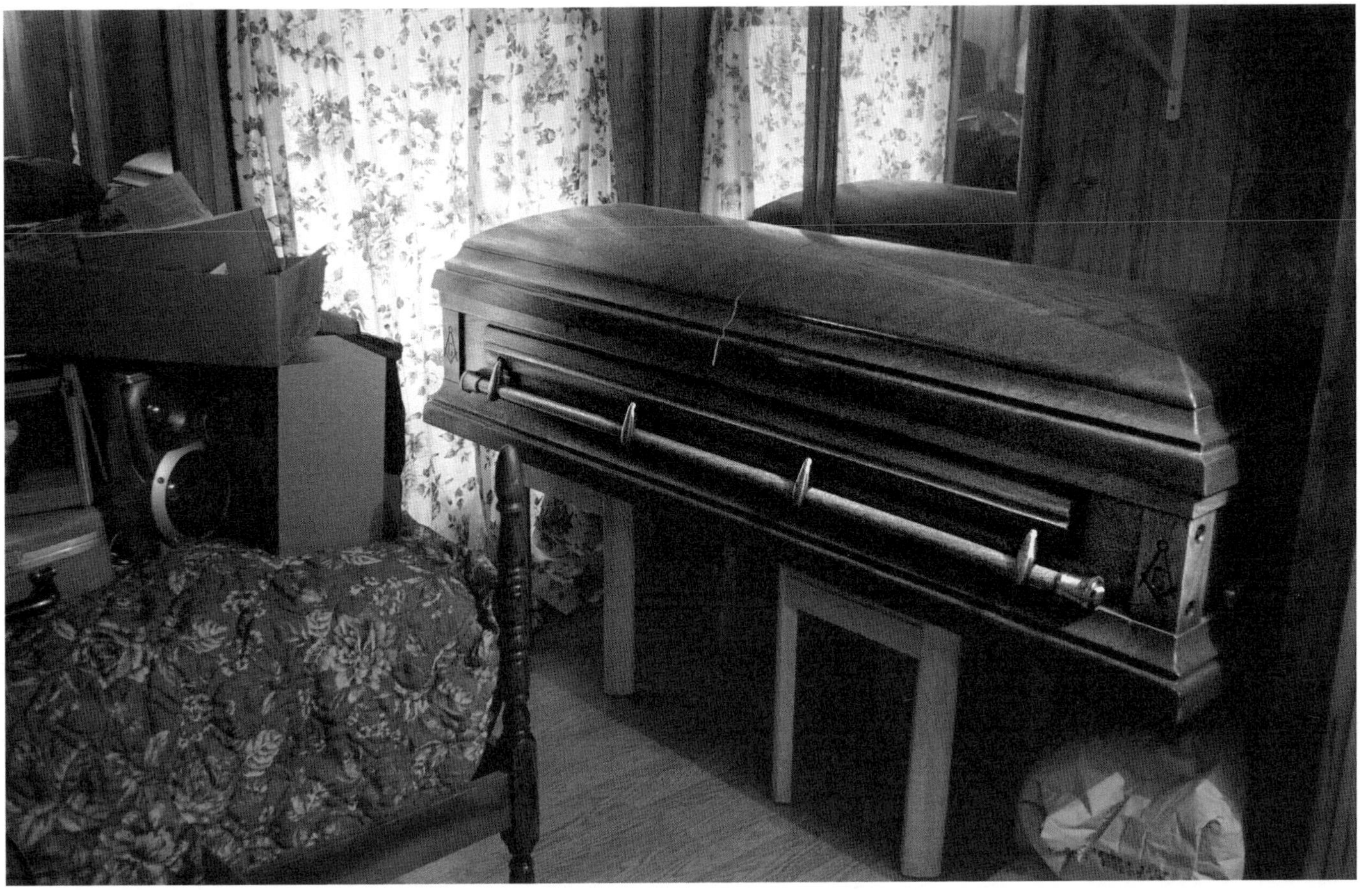

Popcorn's Coffin in His Bedroom

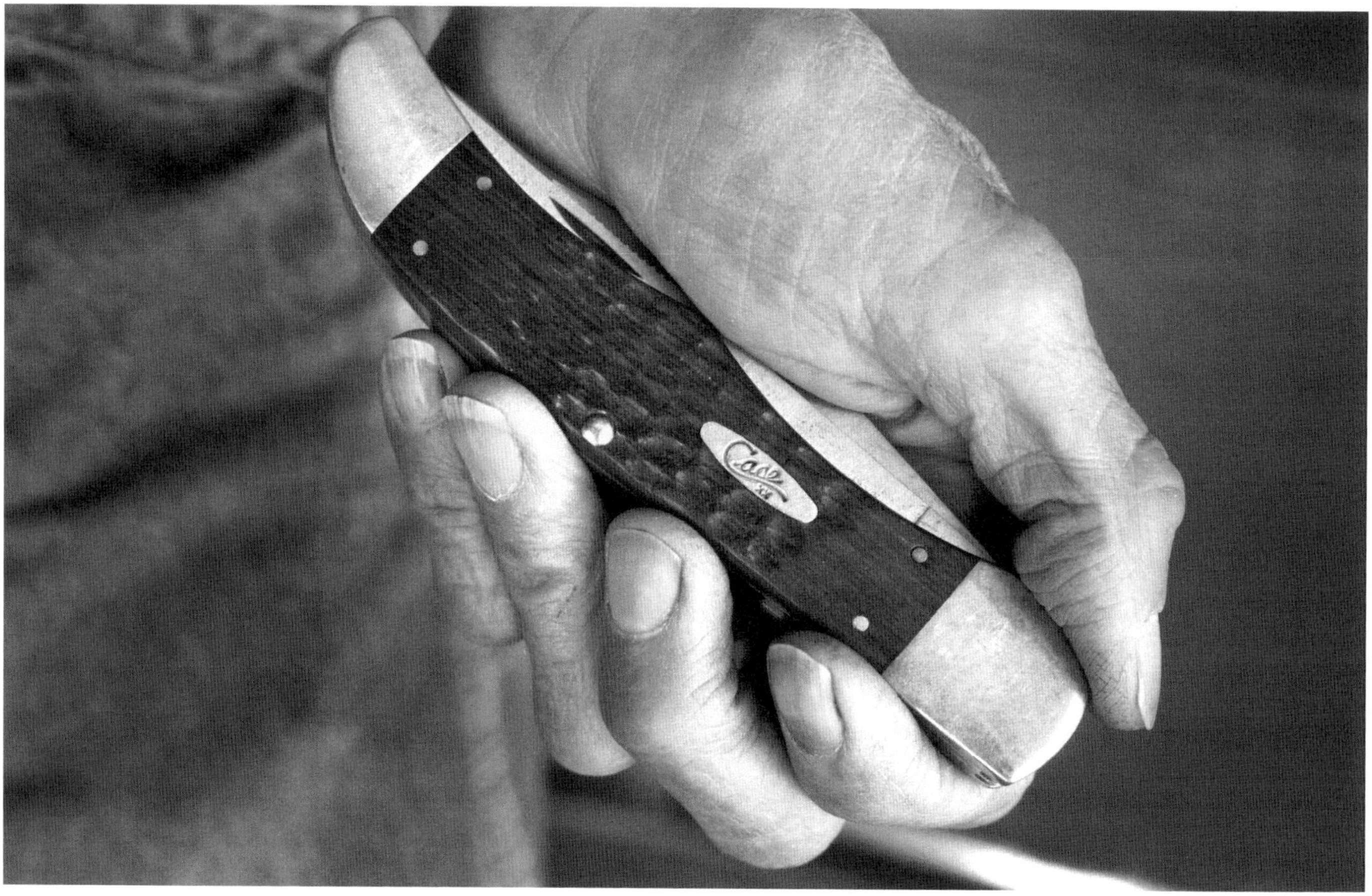

Popcorn's Favorite Trapper Knife

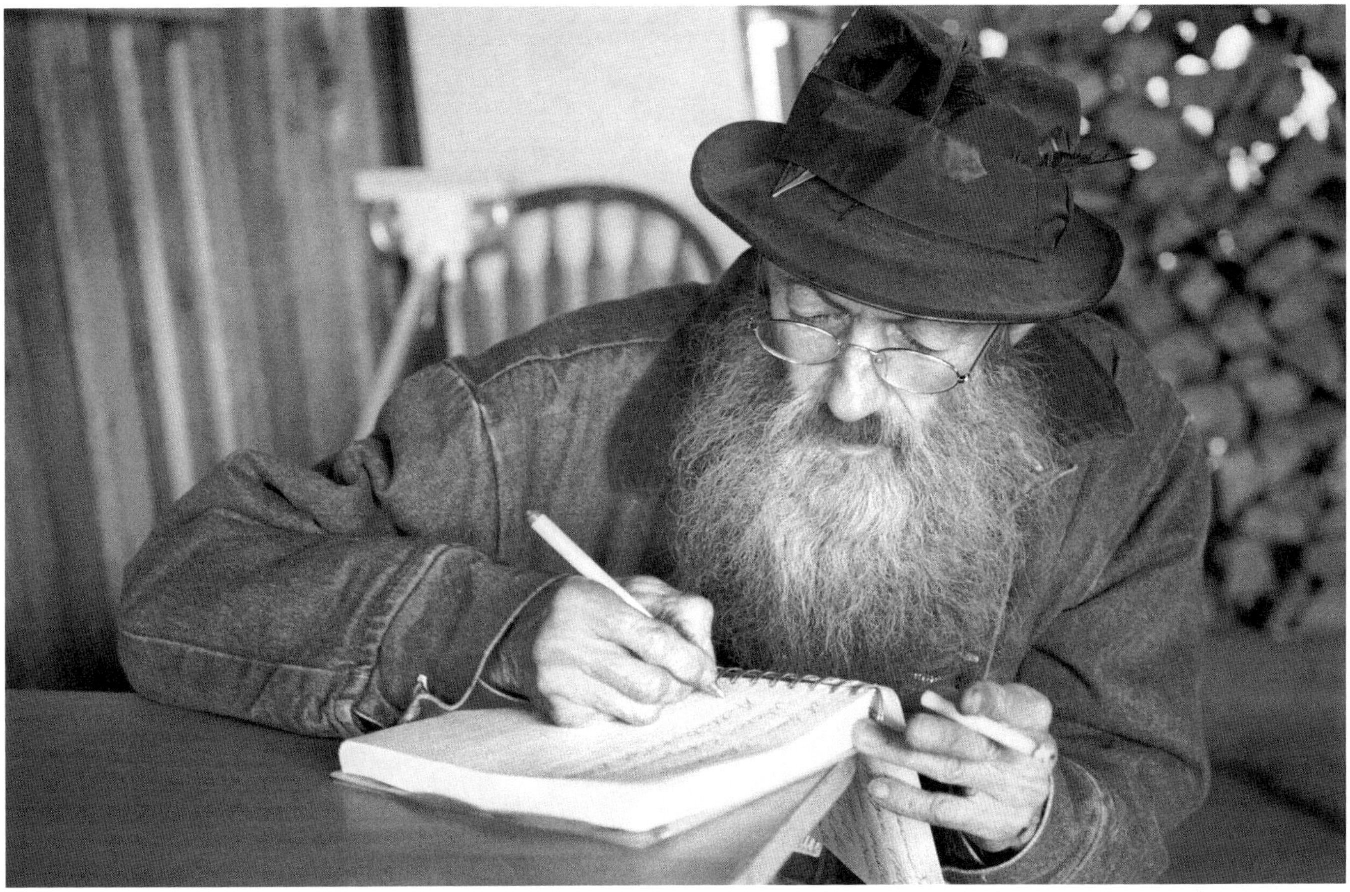

Writing the Recipe for Making “Likker”

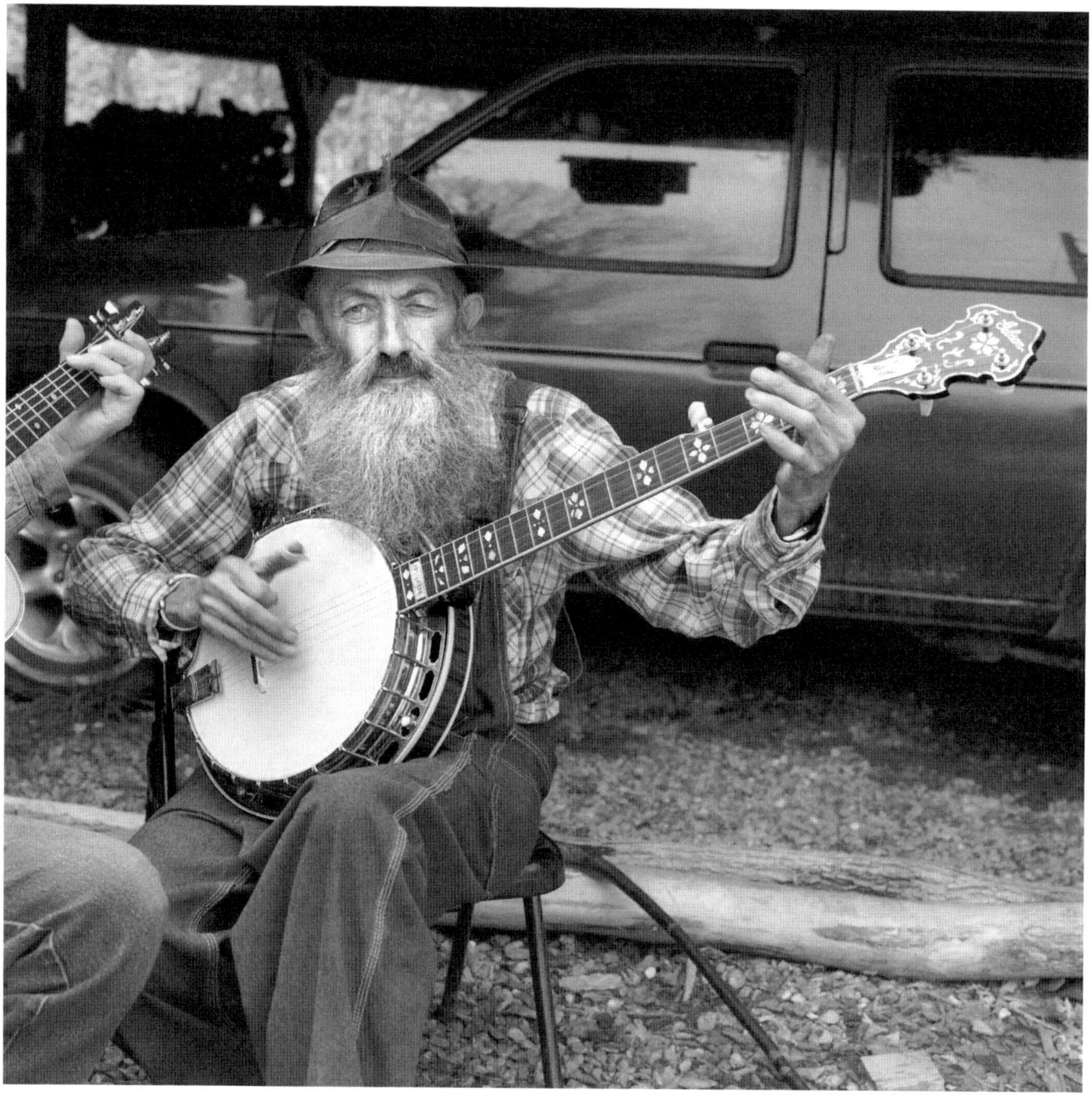

Popcorn "Playing" His Custom Gold Banjo

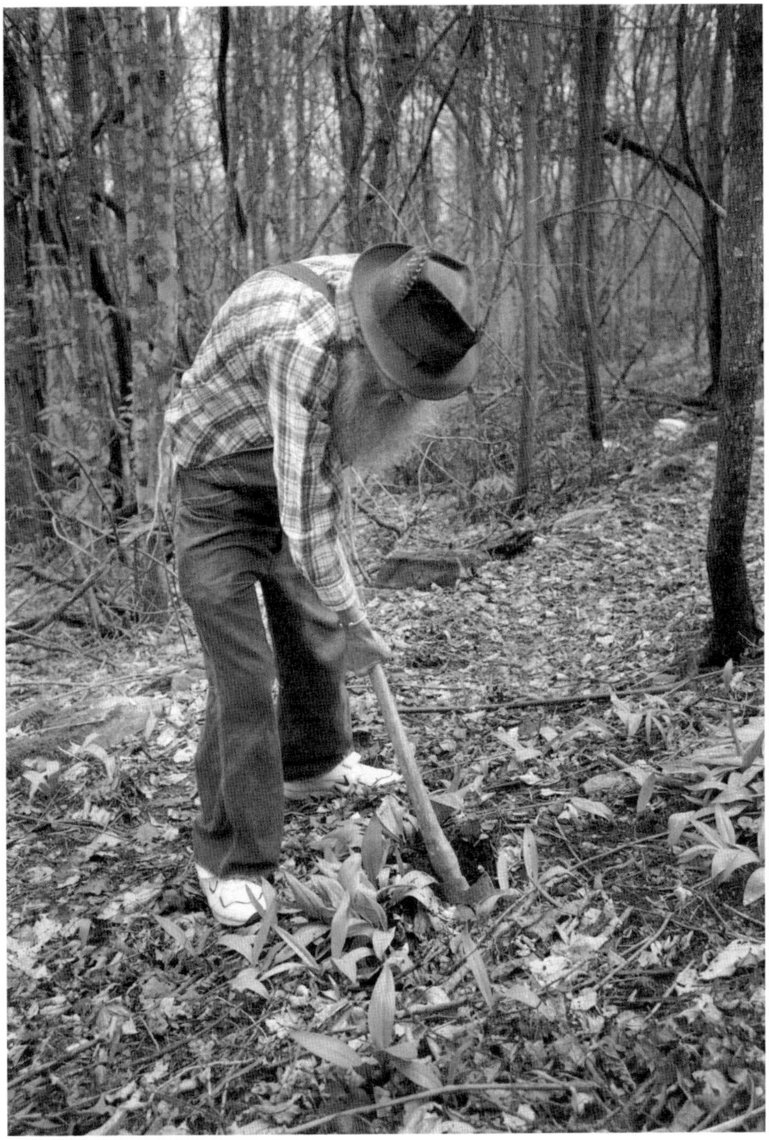

Digging Ramps for Dinner

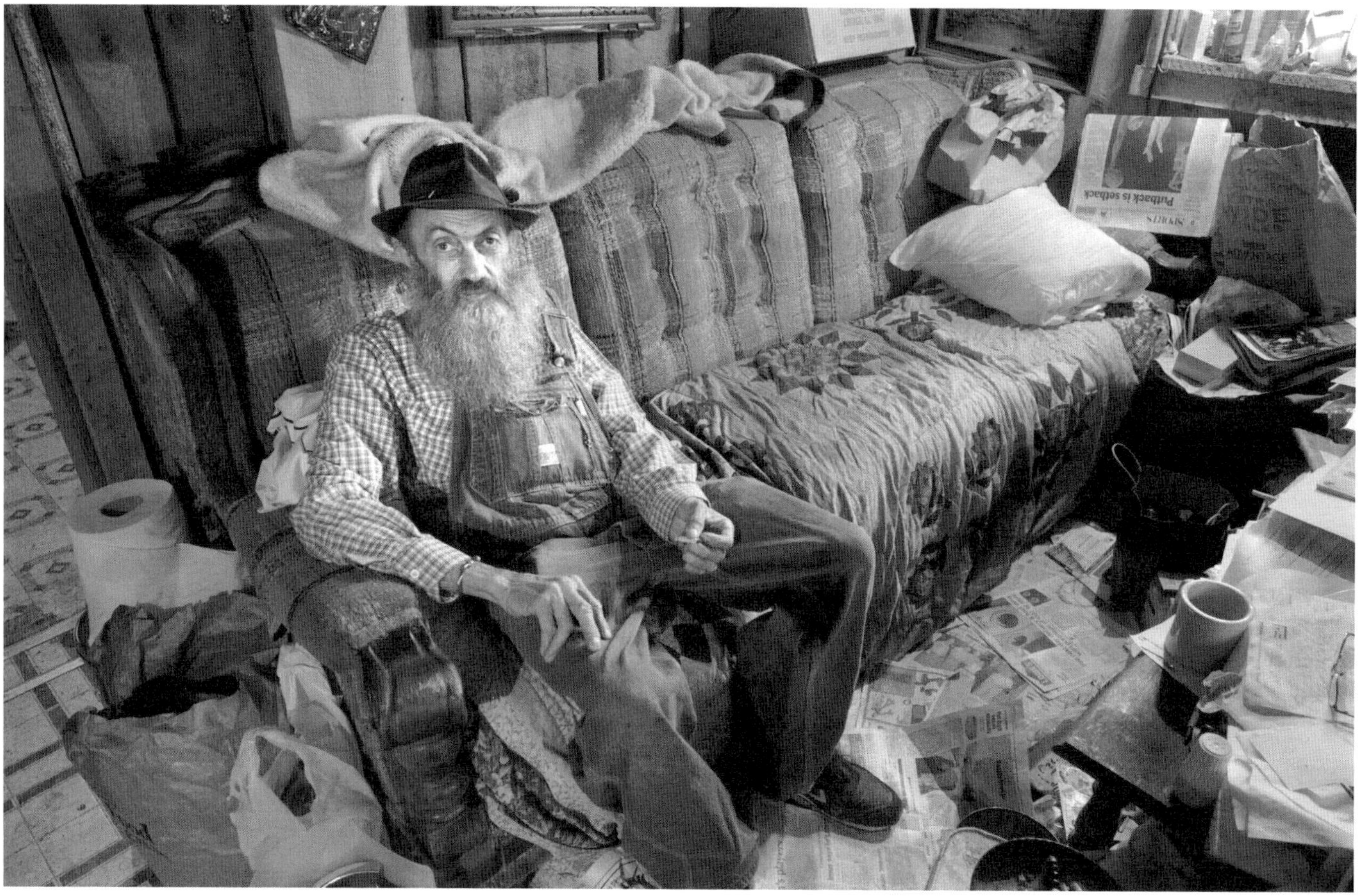

Inside the Original House

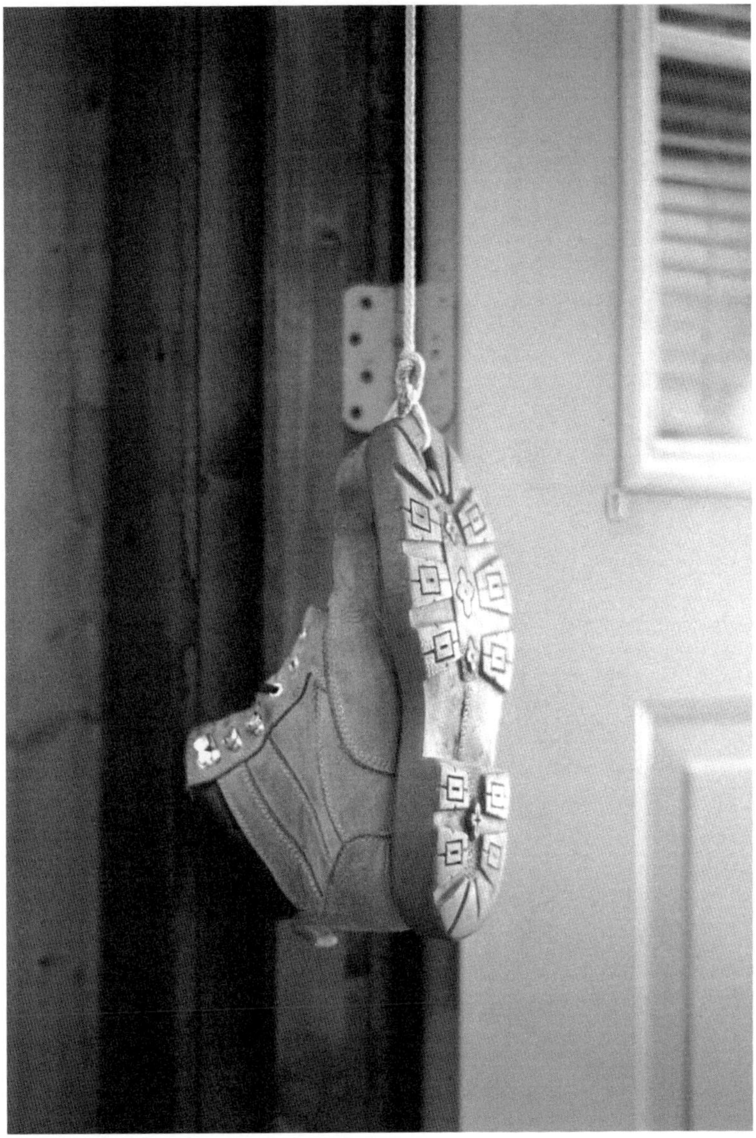

Part of Popcorn's Sexual Pleasure Machine

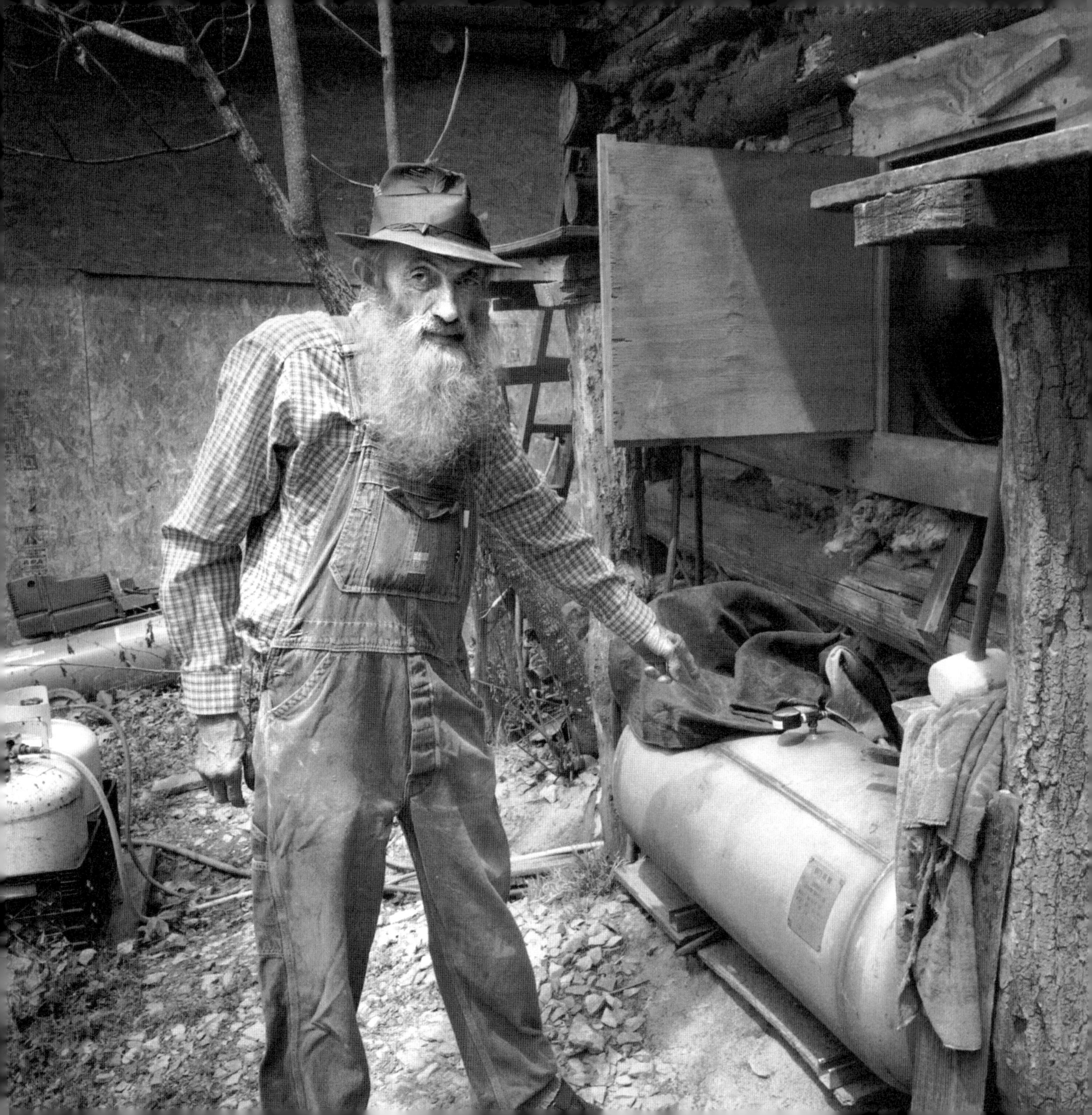

"If you're afraid of this shit, you shouldn't be a-doin' it,"

- Popcorn Sutton

FINALLY, WE GOT down to business and Popcorn took Don and me up to his still house and introduced us to his still hands where the day's run was in process. Don was going to photograph the run and I was going to record audio.

Popcorn's only rules:

- Don't ask the still hands their last names.
  They're to be known only as "Big Dave" and "Billy the Kid."
- Photograph anything inside the still house, but nothing on the outside because of the county election posters on the door.

We followed the process step-by-step around the three big pots. One of them, the one Popcorn called "the grandaddy of "em all" held 160 barrels, according to Popcorn. It's possible that Popcorn was exaggerating – it wouldn't be out of character for him to do that – but standard whiskey barrels hold 49 gallons, so that's 7,840 gallons. Even if the still held between 500 and 1,000 gallons, which is more likely, it would seem clear that whatever the quantity, Popcorn wasn't making whiskey for a hobby; this was a serious commercial operation. His pots were not made of copper, but of stainless steel. Copper pots produce better whiskey, but they're smaller and not good for mass production. Food grade stainless steel, the kind Popcorn used, are not only better for mass production, they make moonshine that's safer to drink. The galvanized steel used in the "silver cloud" stills, in combination with the lead used in the soldered joints, produce moonshine that's about as safe to drink as iodine. "I don't fool with no silver cloud myself," Popcorn said. "Cause that shit'll eat you up."

Popcorn salvaged the stainless steel pots he used for his big still from an old Stokely bean processing plant in nearby Newport, the county seat of Cocke County.

"Billy the Kid" was a friendly, gentle soul, very proud of the job he did and happy to talk freely about it. He said he didn't drink moonshine himself, but a lot of people did, sometimes as part of a home remedy for colds and sore throat. Soak hard candy in a jar of moonshine, he explained, and use the saturated sweets in place of store-bought cough drops. To take the pain away from a baby who's teething, Billy said, "You just dip your finger into some moonshine and rub it on the baby's sore gums. Lotta people do that."

If you do want to consume it, there's also a relatively painless way of drinking moonshine, at least at first. Heat it on a stove and mix it with apple juice, honey, cinnamon and ginger. This is called "apple pie." Other variations on this theme are called by whatever fruit is used for a flavor base. "Peach pie," for example.

Billy said making moonshine and selling it was just a way for a lot of folks to make a living "and take care of our moms and dads, and we all take care of Popcorn," said Billy. "He's a good 'un."

MOONSHINE ETIQUETTE EXPLAINED

THAT DAY AT THE STILL was the day I learned how to drink moonshine. I don't mean the technique for drinking it. That's obvious when you take your first sip – you drink it carefully and very slowly. Keep it in your freezer (no way that much alcohol will turn to ice) and, Big Dave told us, "don't mix it with nothin." It's not the technique for drinking moonshine I'm talking about – the need to drink it slowly is evident with the first sip – but the protocol for drinking moonshine, what you're supposed to say when you try someone's shine for the first time. It's like a wine tasting, when you're supposed to say something hyperbolic like, "a brave little varietal, but I find its presumption as refreshing as the taste." That wouldn't work at a moonshine tasting.

When sampling a moonshiner's product, after taking your first sip, and after a thoughtful pause to allow your tongue and your breath to recover, you need say only one word to be correct: "Smooth."

That's all the moonshiner wants to hear.

I wish I'd known that when the camo pants NASCAR waitress said to Don and me, "Ye ain't from around here, are you?" If I'd just answered "smooth!" everything would've been fine from then on.

When Billy was capping the jugs later (with the brand new caps insisted on by the master, Popcorn himself) he said, "you might wonder why I'm puttin' these caps on so fast. Well, it's because if you don't, they'll be a gnat in there 'fore ye know it."

"Yeah, a dog pecker gnat," Big Dave added for clarification.

When we got a chance to talk to Big Dave about matters other than dog pecker gnats, he said he didn't mind being interviewed, as long as he didn't have to stop working ("I'm a doer not a talker," he said.) But he wouldn't allow himself to be photographed.

As he was filling jugs with moonshine using what looked like a gas pump nozzle, he told me how he'd been involved with moonshining since he was 12, doing one of the most basic and backbreaking jobs in the business – "carryin' sugar." "I was as big then as I am now and strong as a mule," he said.

Big Dave was certainly big, and no doubt very strong. He was also no stranger to the dark side of the law, which probably accounted for his unwillingness to be photographed, a speculation that would become troubling later on.

Don and I followed Popcorn as he was lighting burners and capping the pots. Don with his camera and I with my recorder were trying hard not to trip as we stepped over propane gas hoses fueling the hellish heat of the big burners in the still house.

"If you're afraid of this shit, you shouldn't be a-doin' it," Popcorn told us, as he explained how the burners were first fired off with car gas to heat them up and make the propane burn better. The gas and propane came from tanks outside.

Popcorn said he'd been "blowed up" a time or two while lighting the burners, one time catching his beard on fire. "Ever since then it won't grow no farther than right here," he said, using his hand to indicate "right here" at the end of a grey confusion of a beard that couldn't quite make its way to the top of the bib on his overalls.

Later that day, when the run was almost finished, Don and I had a moment to talk with Big Dave. That's when things began to get a little scary and a lot more strange than even Popcorn's commode portrait.

Billy's way of "looking out for Popcorn" was kind-hearted and respectful. Kind of sweet, really.

Dave's way of looking after Popcorn was more like the way a thuggish bodyguard would do it. Nothing sweet about it at all.

Dave told us he knew how to kill people and had the equipment to do it. If he couldn't cut someone "slap in two" with his knife, he could use the Colt Python .357 magnum revolver he showed us. That's a big pistol not really designed for target practice. It's usually carried by police who might need a .357 magnum round to drop a man or stop a car by shooting through the engine block.

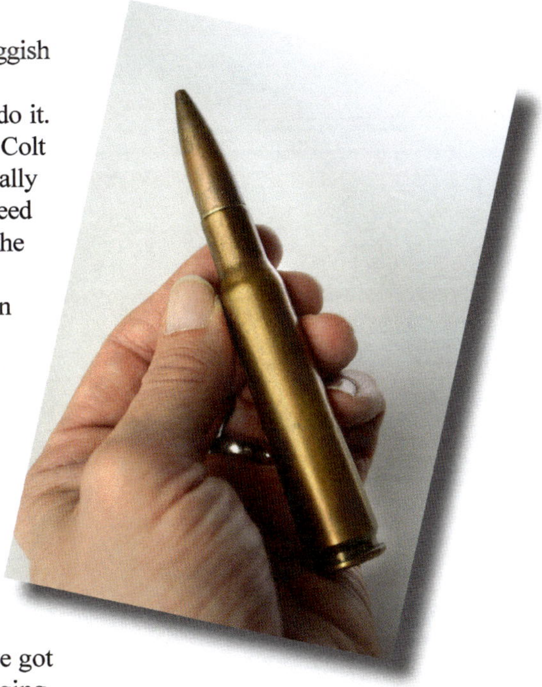

Big Dave went back to his truck and brought back his really big gun for show and tell.

"You know about guns don't you?" Big Dave asked, not waiting for an answer before he showed us his big rifle. It looked like some kind of "elephant gun" to me, but I later learned it was Barrett .50-caliber sniper rifle, the kind they use in the military. The .50 caliber round it fires – it's about five and a half inches long overall – was originally designed for heavy machine guns in World War I. Fired from a scope-mounted sniper rifle, a .50 caliber can easily take a man down at 2,000 yards, and Big Dave said he could do it, too.

After that little pep talk from Big Dave, who was getting scarier by the minute, Don and I started thinking maybe it was time we got the hell outta there. All that bad-ass talk could've been just redneck bragging. On the other hand, Big Dave really didn't have the look of someone who'd be bluffing about what he could do if provoked, and did we really want to take that chance? Uh, no.

Don and I made some kind of excuse, like "we've got all we need for today" and headed back out another side road leading out of Popcorn's property. About halfway down the road Don's cell phone rang. It was Popcorn asking us to come back because he had something he wanted us to help him with. I didn't even have time to ask Don the usual question reserved for times like that: Dudenbostel, what have you gotten us into this time?

We took a deep breath and turned back to help Popcorn put down a rug in his house. Very neatly, as Popcorn instructed, and lined up just right. Then we left and headed to our houses. Finally.

Popcorn left right after we did to go pick up wedding invitations at the printer. He was getting married soon, and that's what people who are getting married do. Sounds very normal, doesn't it? Except that most happy bridegrooms-to-be don't leave behind about 1,000 gallons of highly flammable pure grain alcohol sitting next to several tanks and containers of propane and car gas.

While Popcorn was away from the still house something happened.

AGED MOONSHINE?

POPCORN HAD some whiskey he made that he'd aged in oak barrels, like they do legal whiskey, and had some more he'd made into what he called "apricot brandy." Popcorn's apricot brandy moonshine certainly sounded smoother, almost delicate, but I have my doubts if its presumption would be as refreshing as its taste.

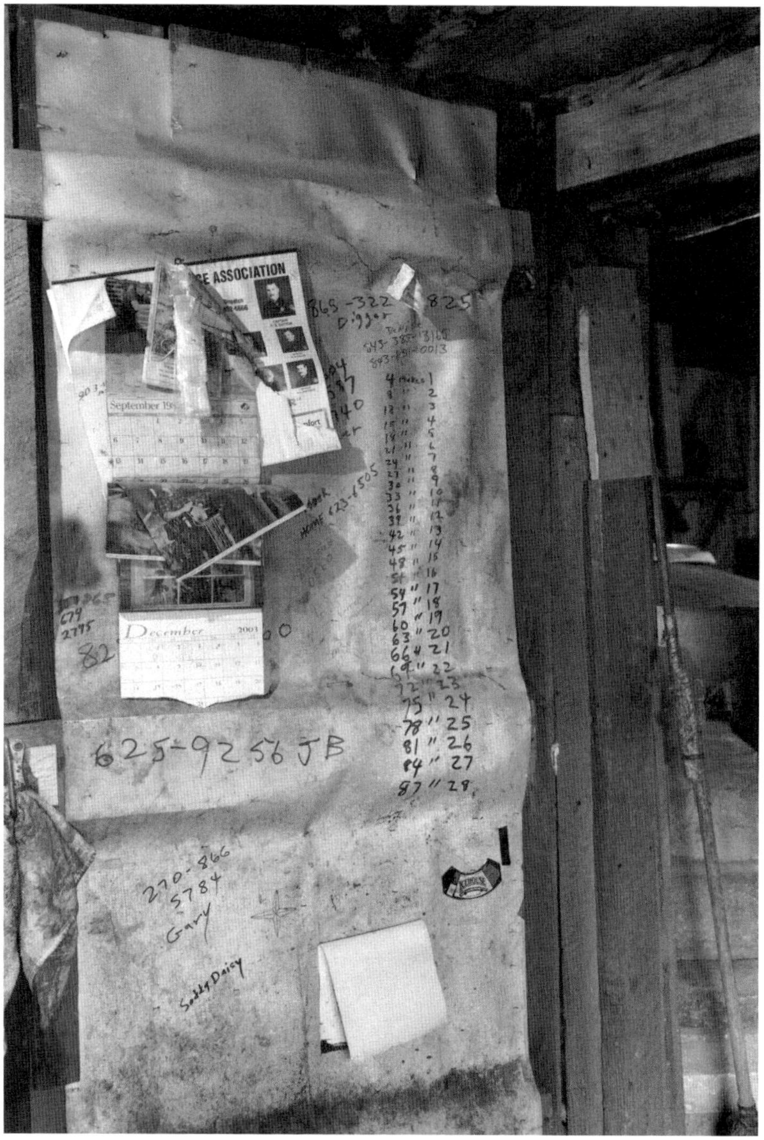

Keeping Track of the "Likker" Run

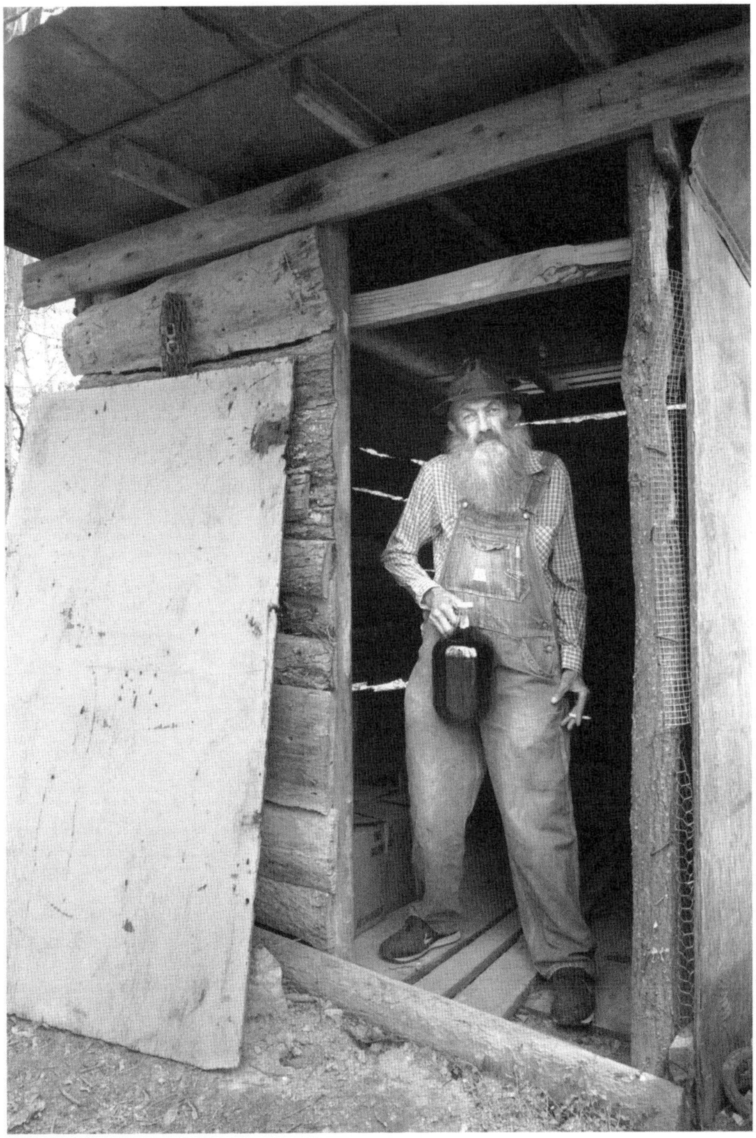

"Aged" Moonshine

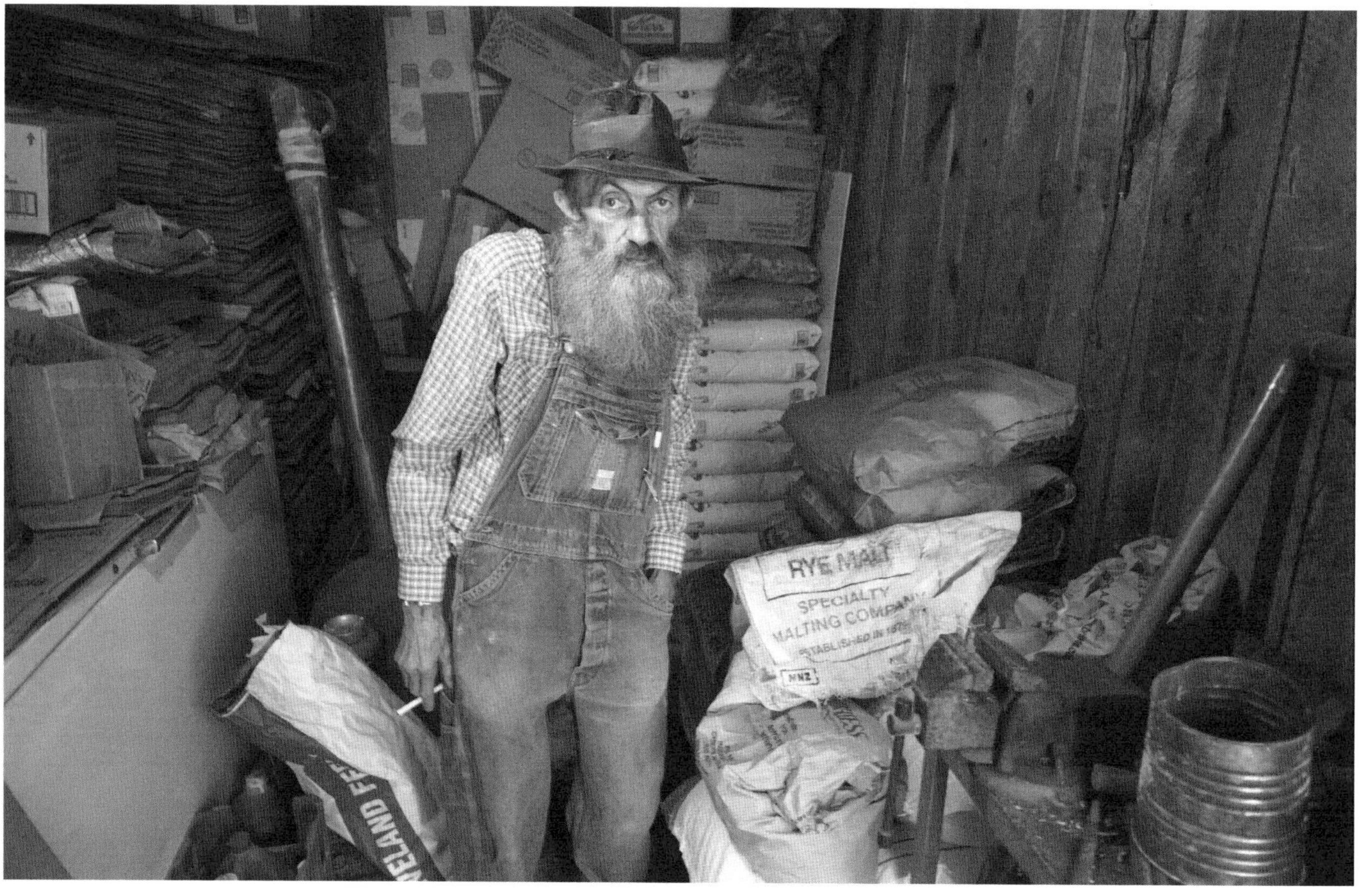

Only the Finest Ingredients

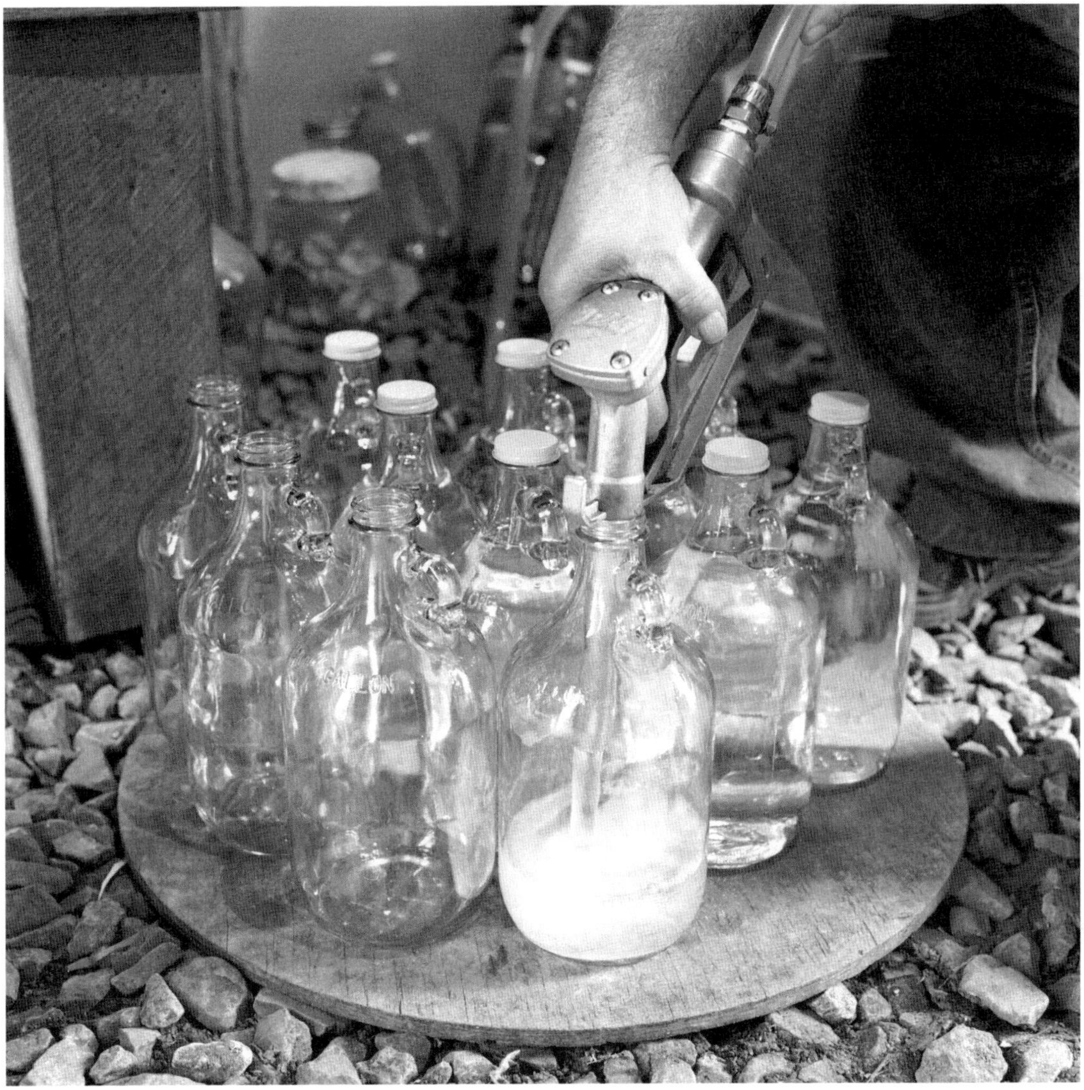

Juggin' It Up

HOW A STILL WORKS

WE LEARNED A LOT about the distillation process from Popcorn which really did help us understand what we were seeing that day at the still house. It's actually a process that involves a lot of science, although the terms used in moonshining sound more folksy than scientific.

A still, illegal or otherwise, operates by a process of evaporation (encouraged by heat from burners under the pot) and condensation. You get the cold condensate from the "worm" or copper coil in the thumper keg or from the "shotgun", a newer type of condenser that doesn't use a worm coil. Distillation takes out impurities and condenses the volume of the liquid in the pot. The alcohol that results from the distillation of corn mash comes from the natural fermentation of sugar and mash over time.

A pot still, the kind Popcorn used, is not as pure as a reflux still used for more scientific purposes, but it produces a more flavorful whiskey.

There are a lot of impurities in the first run, like methanol, isopropyl and some harmful ketones. That's the way the substances are described in organic chemistry terms, but in moonshining terms it means that bad stuff made with only profit in mind can REALLY hurt you. And not just with a dreadful hangover, either; bad moonshine can kill you.

Popcorn started his first run, which took about two hours. Then, when it was completed, he threw it away ("nigger whiskey," he called it, deeming it not fit to drink but possibly useful to clean out a thumper keg). He knew when he discarded that first run, he got rid of a lot of the bad stuff, like the starches that are in the grain that convert to methanol, or sugars that convert into ethanol. He didn't explain it that way, but "bad stuff" is close enough.

The first fermentation is called "sweet mash." That's the bad stuff. The next fermentations after that are called "sour mash." That's what you want if you're trying to make the best moonshine. Old-timers used to mark the jugs with an X for first run, two Xs for the second run and three Xs for the more desirable third run. That's where the "XXX" marking on old moonshine jugs comes from.

The second run of the still, the run that Popcorn keeps and doesn't throw away, is not smooth. "Top shots," the moonshiner's term for what comes out of the still first, are not meant to be smooth. Top shots are almost 190 proof, or pure grain alcohol. That clear and potent liquid is not meant to be consumed, but mixed with "backins" from subsequent runs.

As these runs finish, Popcorn fills the jugs with the distillate as it comes off the still. The jugs first in line are the most potent, with potency decreasing in order as subsequent jugs are filled and put in line. What Popcorn calls "backins" are the jugs at the back end of the line. These are the jugs he mixes with the first runs to "temper down" the mix and dilute it to as close to 100 proof as possible. The

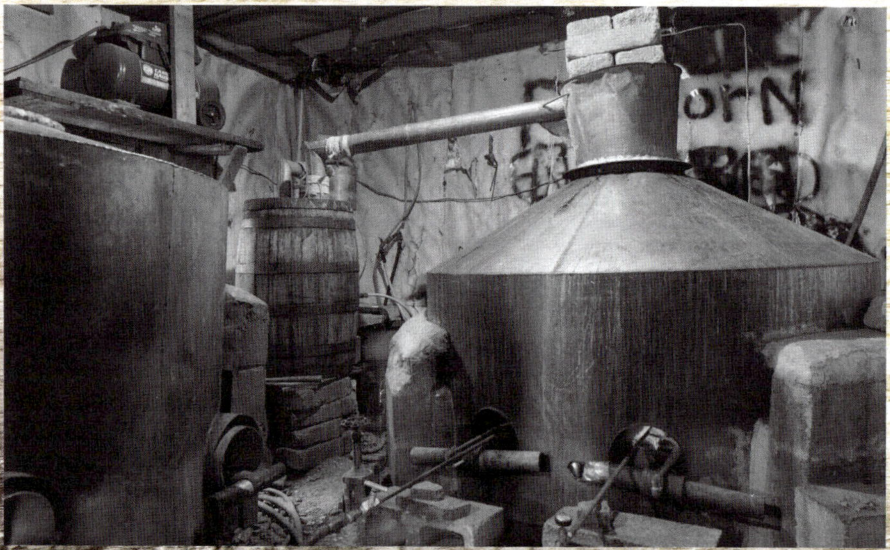

result is firewater that's anywhere between 100 and 120 proof.

You know when you've tempered the moonshine down to the 100 proof range that's considered drinkable when you see how it "beads up." Popcorn told us that when you turn a jar of moonshine over to look at the bubbles, or "beads," you've got it "right at" 100 proof when "it's half big 'uns and half little 'uns."

"This is where the experience comes in," Popcorn said, but he allowed that Big Dave was getting the hang of it and expressed that thought in pure Appalachian mountain dialect: "He's cotched on faster'n any man I've ever seed."

There is another use for top shots, though, besides using it as a base making the tempered whiskey. You use the 190-proof top shots to make what Popcorn called "kick ass cherries." This is a pint jar full of 190 proof loaded up with maraschino cherries. You don't drink the stuff, just eat the kick-ass cherries to get the desired effect. Besides getting you real drunk in a hurry, kick-ass cherries can also make real purty puke.

What I'm not sure about is that I'd recommend drinking moonshine for any reason, smooth or not. Even the best and smoothest moonshine in the world, which Popcorn's presumably was, "will knock ye on ye aise and tell ye what fer later." That's one of the many colorful descriptions Popcorn used to describe the effect his product could have. Another way of saying it is that even the best moonshine in the world is still moonshine, and that stuff can hit you hard.

As for me, just to digress a bit, I had an experience with Popcorn's moonshine that caused me to go face down on a dinner table one night. After grilling steaks and trading shots with a friend of mine who's a lot bigger than I am, I toppled over like a tree blown down in a windstorm. My friend went down, too; it just took him longer to fall down. I was told later the steaks were grilled to perfection, although I have no idea of how I managed to do that or cook anything but my brain. After that experience, I swore off any further experimentation with moonshine.

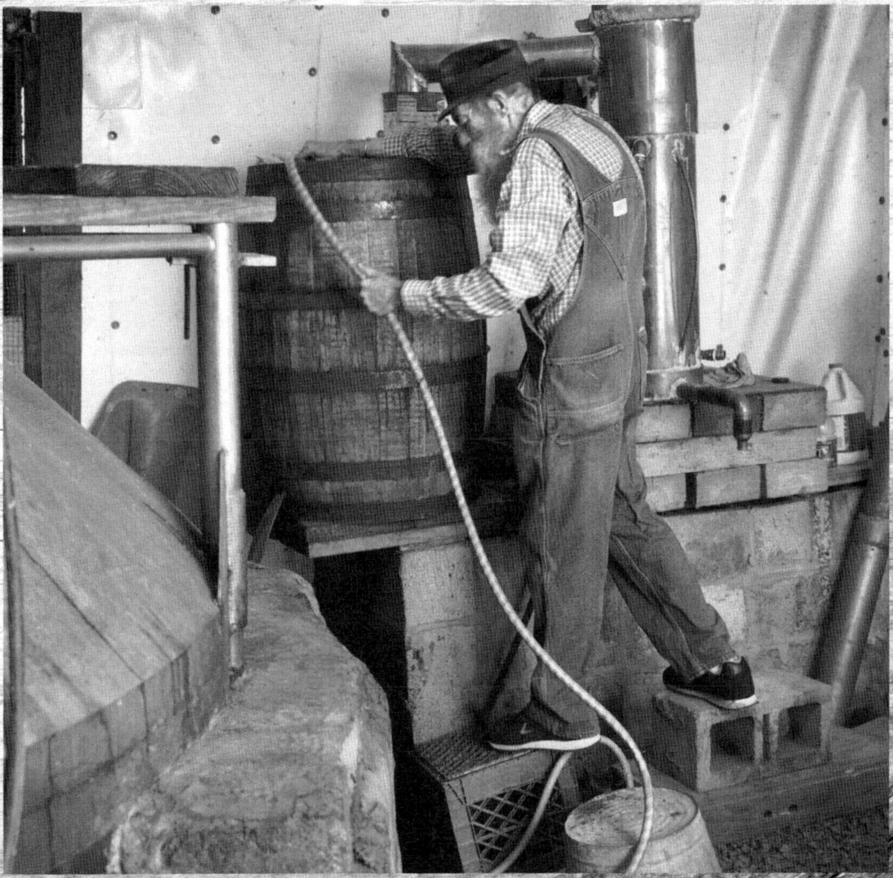

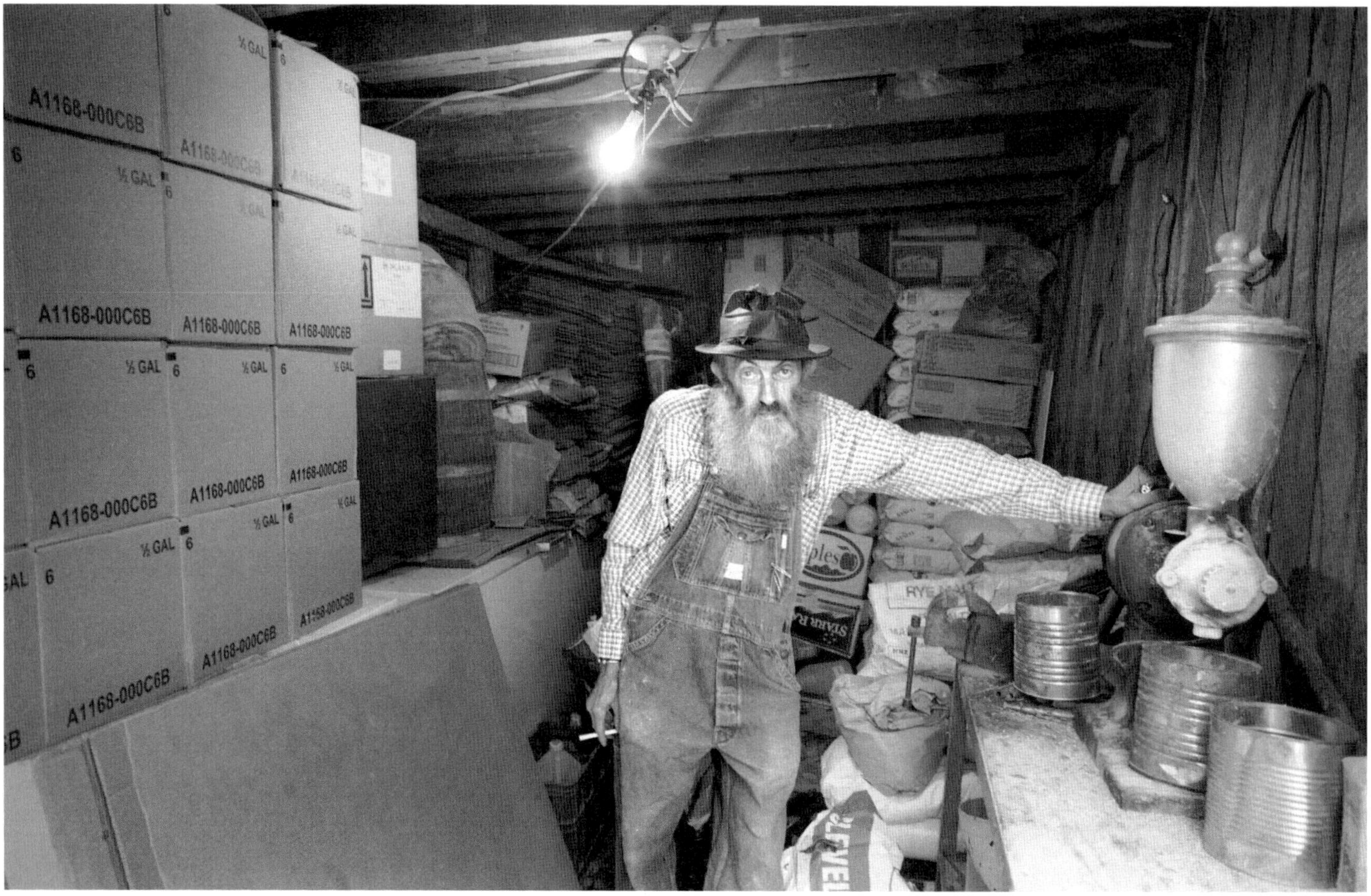

Popcorn's 1948 A&P Coffee Grinder Used to Grind the Corn

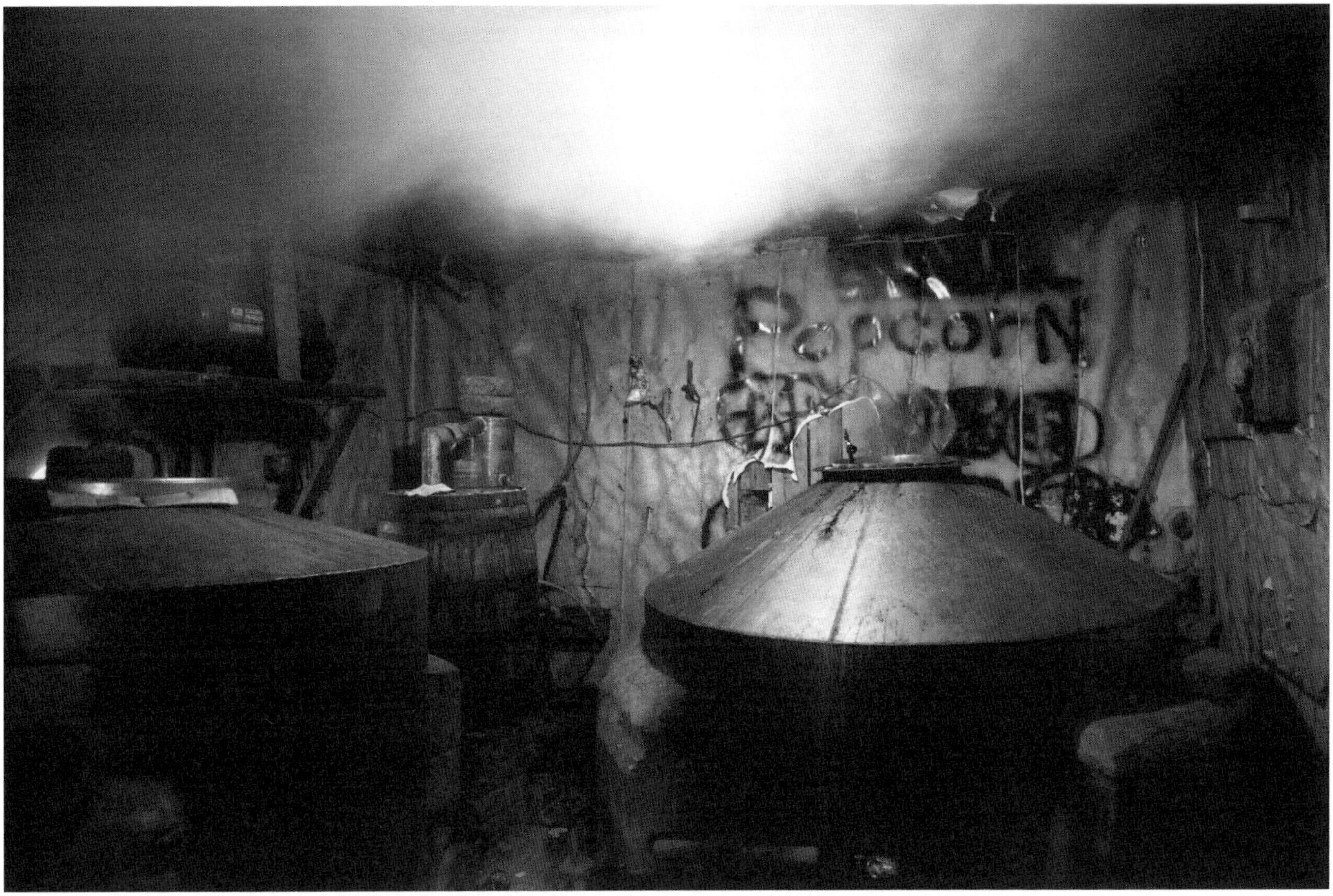

Steam Escapes After Still is Opened From a Run

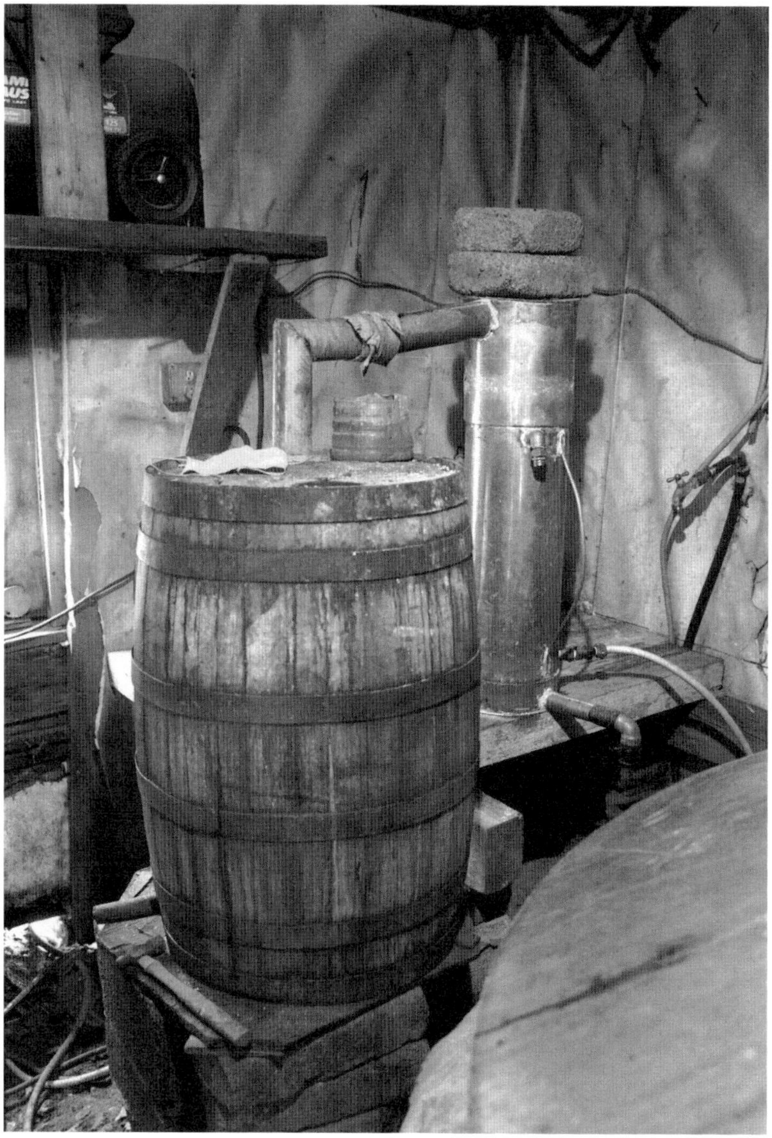

Thumper Keg and Shotgun Condenser

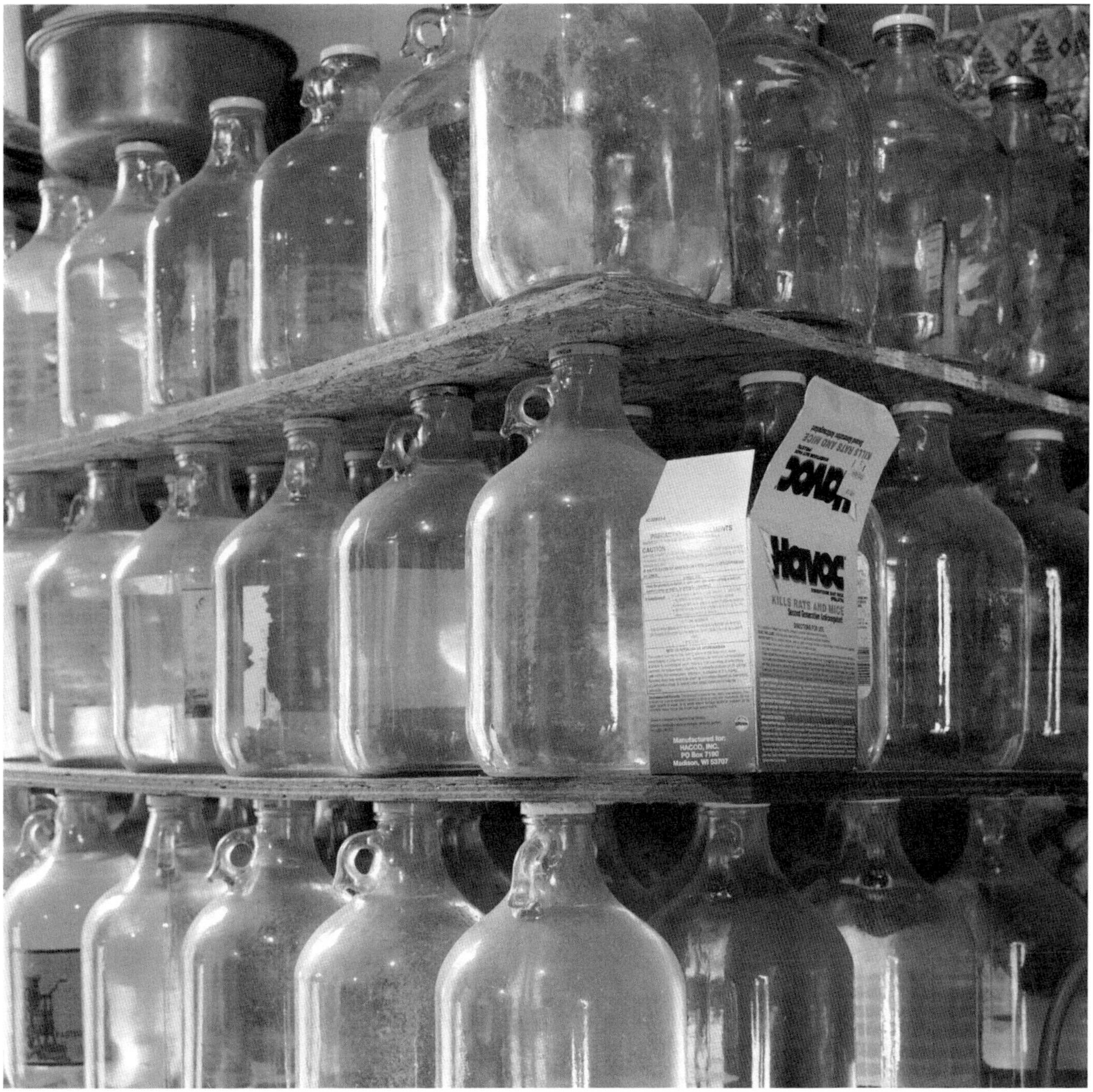

"Backins" - The Tail End of a Run

MOONSHINE MARKETING 101

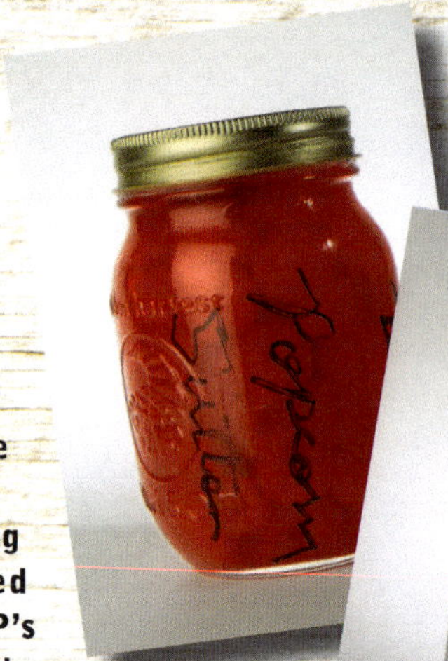

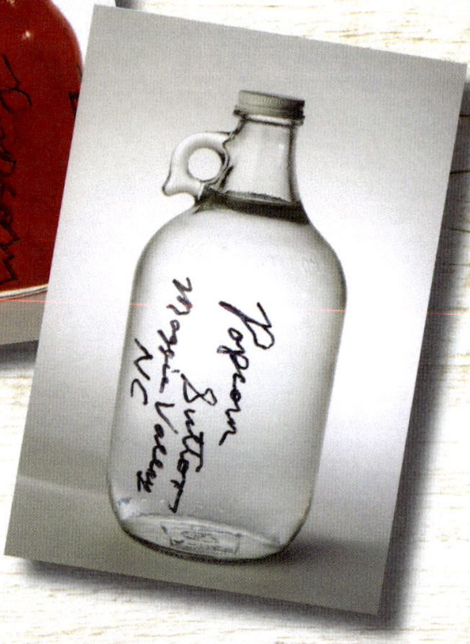

LISTEN UP, YOUNG 'UNS, this is how Popcorn Sutton did it, and what your big city marketing department can learn from an old moonshiner who was as good at selling his product as he was at making it.

Moonshining may be a shady, if revered, tradition in Appalachia, but Popcorn Sutton was able to look way beyond the tradition to understand that he was also in the business of manufacturing and distributing a product. Popcorn's method of marketing the moonshine he made was successful by any measure and would be the envy of any brand or marketing manager.

When you get down to it and look beyond the tradition, moonshining is still a product manufactured and sold. Illegal, yes, but a product nonetheless, to be marketed like any other. That's exactly what Popcorn did, using his own version of established marketing principles.

Popcorn was not a highly educated man in the formal sense. He made it to the 10th grade before he dropped out of school to pursue his real passion, which was moonshining. "It's all I ever thought about, was moonshining," Popcorn said. Following in the footsteps of his father and grandfather, he just couldn't wait to get started.

As he refined his manufacturing process, that is, as he got better at making "quality" moonshine, he got better at selling it. How did he do it? Really, just by applying the simple basics of marketing.

The American Marketing Association has standardized this process as the "4 P's of marketing". This is the "marketing mix" model that's been around since the 1940s, when a marketing professor named James Culliton described the marketing manager as a "mixer of ingredients." He had no idea how true that would be with Popcorn Sutton.

Another marketing professor, E. Jerome McCarthy, later bottled Culliton's "ingredients" into the groups we now know as the "4 P's." In no particular order, they are Price, Product, Place and Promotion.

In his own way, Popcorn really did stick to the classic 4 P's. But usually with an unconventional difference, starting with the sometimes problematic fact that his product was illegal and getting caught making it or selling it could land you in jail. That's why there are more notorious moonshiners than there are notorious marketers.

He established a **PRICE** based on how much he knew moonshiner consumers would pay and still come back for more -- $25 for a half-gallon. But Popcorn established the price for his product with one big difference: he knew how much a customer would pay drunk for a jug of moonshine without starting a fight. People who make and sell baby formula rarely have that problem.

Popcorn made moonshining a respected job description, at least where he lived, got himself famous and, in spite of his public poor-mouthing to the contrary, made himself a lot of untaxed cash. Popcorn was really proud of the **PRODUCT** he made and was a stickler for consistency. He used only the best ingredients, like importing his malt from

Germany and grinding it himself. He took extra care in the distilling process, using only the second run of mash to get better quality. And he used only glass jugs that had never been touched when it came time to "jug it up" for distribution and sale. He had only disdain for moonshiners who sold their product in plastic milk jugs.

"If you gonna make it, make it first class," according to professor Popcorn. " If you ain't got the proper equipment, the proper know-how and the proper supplies you do not need to be a-fuckin' with this shit, period. If I sell somebody a jar of likker and makes 'em sicker'n hell, they ain't gonna back and see me no more. I want to sell you a jar a'likker and know you're comin' back. I want re-peat business; I don't want a one-time show."

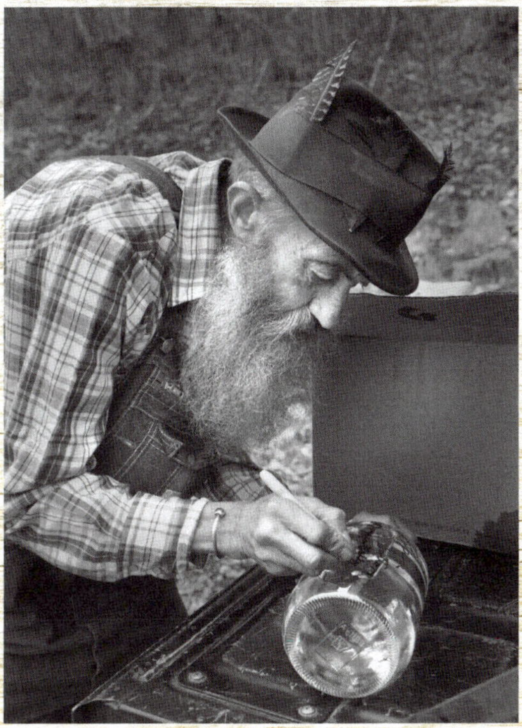

The third P – for **PLACE** – Popcorn adhered to by making his moonshine and selling it in a place where moonshining is in continuous demand and where the authorities many times turn a blind eye to it.

And as for the fourth P – **PROMOTION** -- Popcorn flaunted his trade for all the world to see, and got lots of free press, especially when he got arrested numerous times. Why, up here everybody knows Popcorn Sutton, or at least they say they do, and everybody's got a Popcorn story. That's pure word-of-mouth advertising, the best kind. And for Popcorn it was free. Free, yes, in the sense that it was earned media, but Popcorn's notoriety came with a price. It was, however, a price he was more than willing to pay.

Popcorn knew the difference between Marvin Sutton and Popcorn Sutton is the same as the difference between a jungle and a rain forest: marketing.

If Marvin Sutton was just another mountain man who didn't give a damn about the law, he'd be only another one where there are a lot of 'em. But a mountain man with a long beard running down the high bib of his overalls, who supported the stereotype that we all hate but are somehow proud of, why, that's Popcorn Sutton, and everybody knows Popcorn Sutton.

So there you have it. The four P's of marketing. Except maybe the marketing textbooks could now add a fifth P – for **POPCORN.** What made Popcorn's marketing plan work wasn't that he followed the textbook four P's. What made it work for Popcorn was that he intuitively followed the "rules" of marketing in a way that was totally specific to himself.

If you're someone who drinks moonshine on occasion, you know the more famous and notorious the moonshiner is the more demand there is for his product, even though the manufacturer's image actually has nothing whatsoever to do with the product's quality.

See? Marketing.

And, you'd have to say, Popcorn was a genius at it, developing a marketing strategy that any legal manufacturing business, like, say, the Jack Daniel's distillery over in Lynchburg, might envy.

Well, except for the going to jail part.

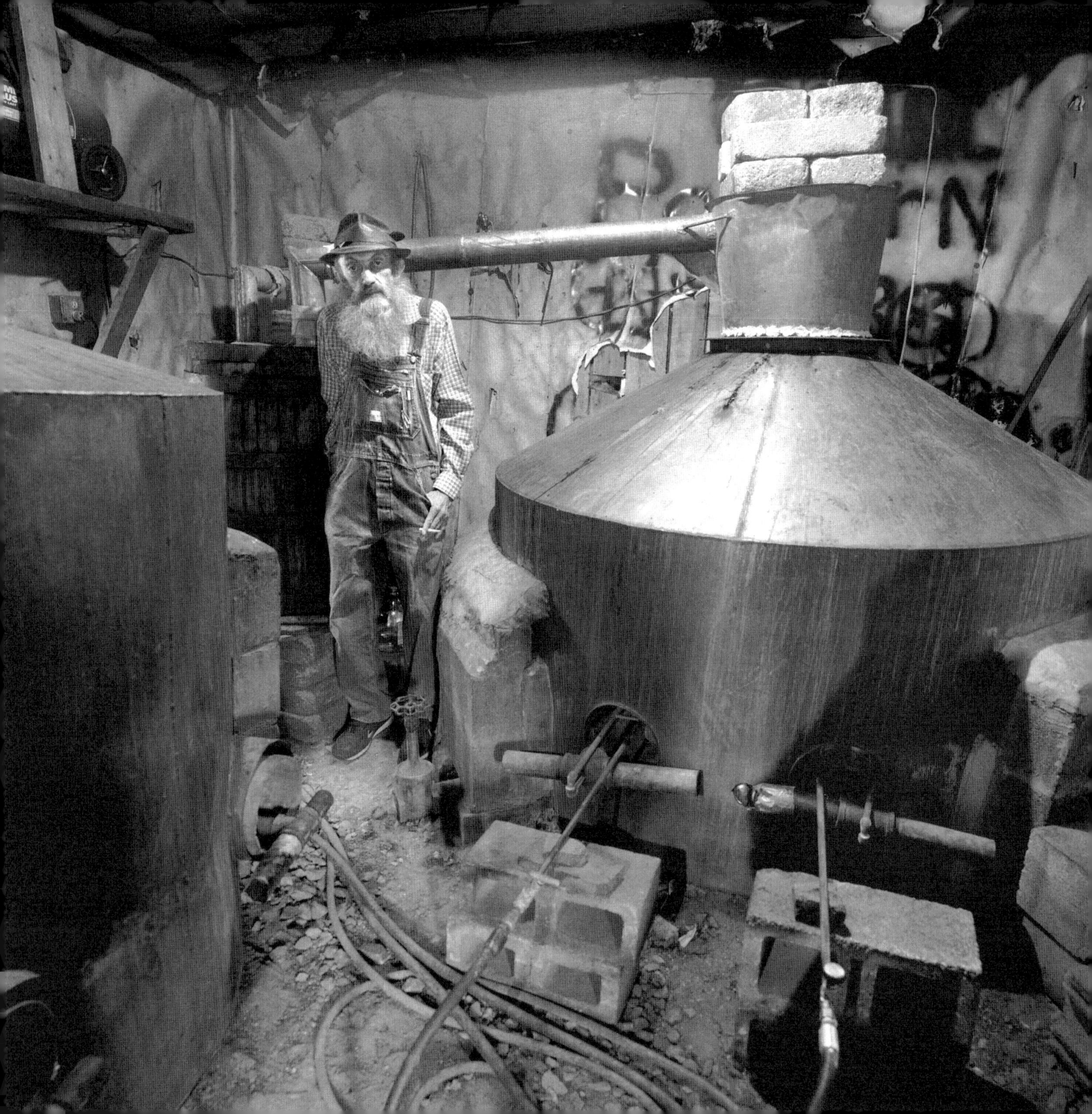

"If you're worried about the law you shouldn't be doin' this. They gonna catch you sooner or later."

– Popcorn Sutton

THERE ARE A LOT of local conspiracy theories around Cocke County about what actually did happen, and conspiracy theories themselves are highly flammable in the jealousy-filled world of the mountain moonshiner. We may never know the full truth but, regardless, something did happen and Popcorn's still house went up in what was probably a giant blue corn-shaped cloud that could be seen for miles.

The fire was just too big to be ignored, so the fire department had to come. Fire departments from both Parrottsville and Cocke County came. Then the law came, even though (Popcorn said) they had orders from county officials to leave him alone (remember the posters on Popcorn's still house door?). They found large amounts of copper tubing and coils, three large stills, a large amount of barley, lots of bags of sugar, glass jugs and caps and confiscating the 37 jugs of finished moonshine. Meanwhile, Popcorn said he was back on his property pulling rolls of large denomination bills out of his overalls and throwing them into the woods. I never heard if anyone ever found the money Popcorn said he tossed into the woods, and he never said anything more about it.

Nobody in Cocke County really wanted to put Popcorn in jail and out of business. So he got probation. Again. Popcorn gave his usual solemn promise that his moonshining days were over for good, "and I mean it this time."

Normally, of course, this would mean that Popcorn would go right back to making moonshine as before, which, of course, he did.

Popcorn never worried too much about getting lawed. It was just the price of doing business to him. I asked him one time, "aren't you worried about getting caught?" He lit another unfiltered cigarette off the one he'd just finished as he talked about how his daddy and granddaddy before him were also moonshiners like him who never gave a damn about the law. "If you're worried about the law you shouldn't be doin' this," he said. "They gonna catch you sooner or later."

The next morning, I got a call from Don about a voicemail message he'd gotten from the previous night. He had his cell phone turned off because he was eating supper and was enjoying the comforts of home, so Don didn't get the call when it came. "Popcorn's been busted," Don said. "His still blew up about an hour after we left."

Don said that Popcorn had left a message to call him as quickly as he could.

So Don called him as quickly as he could.

"He told me he'd been arrested and thrown in jail, and wanted me to put my house up for bail and lend him $10,000 to buy a new still. But he wasn't actually in jail. They'd let him out and he was trying to scam me for my house, a con artist to the end."

Even so, Don and I locked away and hid our photographic and audio evidence for a time, just to be on the safe side and do what they do in Parrottsville, "where everybody looks out for Popcorn."

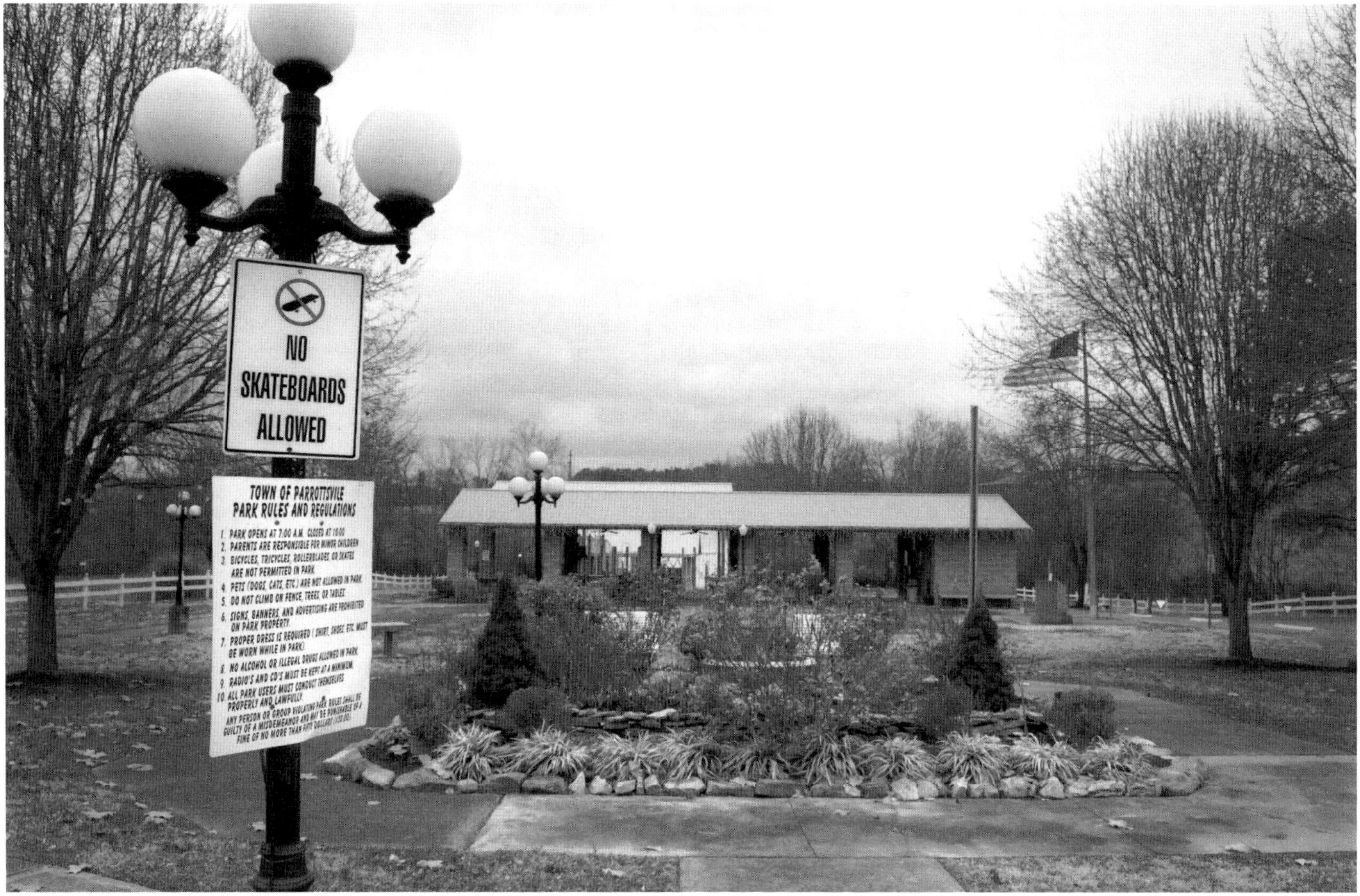

Park in Parrotsville Where Popcorn and Pam Tied the Knot

FOR POPCORN, life went on, not just moonshining, but marrying. While he was out on bond and awaiting trial, Popcorn married the former Pam Manning, who met him when she was cooking at the Country Cafe in Parrottsville. Pam's a great ole country gal with a big family and a big – well, uh, let's just say she's built just the way Popcorn liked for his women to be built. She has a big sweet face, too, and a sweet disposition to go with it. Pam is mountain country to the core, but she's nobody's fool and she has a well-developed streak of Appalachian independence, which she didn't hesitate to bring out when she needed to show Popcorn she wasn't putting up with any more of his ornery ways.

Pam had to work at keeping Popcorn under control, but she was probably the only person who could do it to any extent at all. Underneath the occasional sparring Pam loved that man Popcorn, especially when he revealed to her a very different side of his character during their courting days. Popcorn was at heart a hopeless romantic and courted Pam as a fairy tale knight would court a fairy tale princess. "He was the sweetest, kindest, most loving man I ever met in my life," she said.

"He was very respectful to my family," Pam said. "My family is very important to me, and I've got a big family, but Popcorn did everything just right," she said. "He always put me up on a pedestal."

Here's how Pam told the story of their courtship:

"He came in to the Country Cafe (the restaurant in Parrottsville where Pam was working as a cook) with this birthday card with a receipt inside the fold. I said what's this?

"He said, 'It's your birthday present.' And it's a very lovely card. He was very romantic. But when he signed the card it was very…naisty, but that was just…Popcorn. He had that receipt, he had went and paid my washer and dryer off. Twelve hundred dollars!

"I said, no, no this can't go on! And then I thought, the best way to get rid of him is to introduce him to my family, 'cause I have a BIG family.

"So I told him I'll go to church with you on Easter Sunday, but you have to go to my son's house for dinner afterward. He said all right. I invited my WHOLE family. There were 50 some people there. That backfired royally on me.

"Everyone has lunch and then he gets up and says, 'I need to make an announcement.' And goes to my dad and he says, 'Mr. Manning, I am in love with your daughter, 'and he said, 'I want to marry her and I promise you I will take care of her and she will never want for anything.' And my dad, my whole family, just fell in love with him. And here I am, YOU'RE SUPPOSED TO HELP ME GET RID OF HIM!

"But it didn't work, so I don't know, I don't know what happened. He kept asking me to marry him and I kept telling him no, he didn't know me. I never did say yes. I don't know what happened. We just got married. We met at the end of March and got married on May 13, 2007, on Mother's Day. It was very fast. But I wouldn't trade one minute I've been with that man for anything. He was so good to me."

When Pam and Popcorn got married, they had a very public wedding in Parottsville City Park with lots of people invited and in attendance. At the wedding, Pam wore a white wedding dress and Popcorn dressed the way he always did, in his baggy overalls, long sleeve shirt (he always wore long sleeves to cover a tattoo he wasn't proud of), and his trademark beat-up old brown fedora. On this occasion, however, in a rare burst of propriety -- or maybe because Pam told him to -- Popcorn removed from the hat's crown the delicate part of raccoon anatomy he usually kept there.

The couple didn't get to stay together long, though, because events that were set in motion the day Popcorn's still burned continued to spool out until they reached a shocking end.

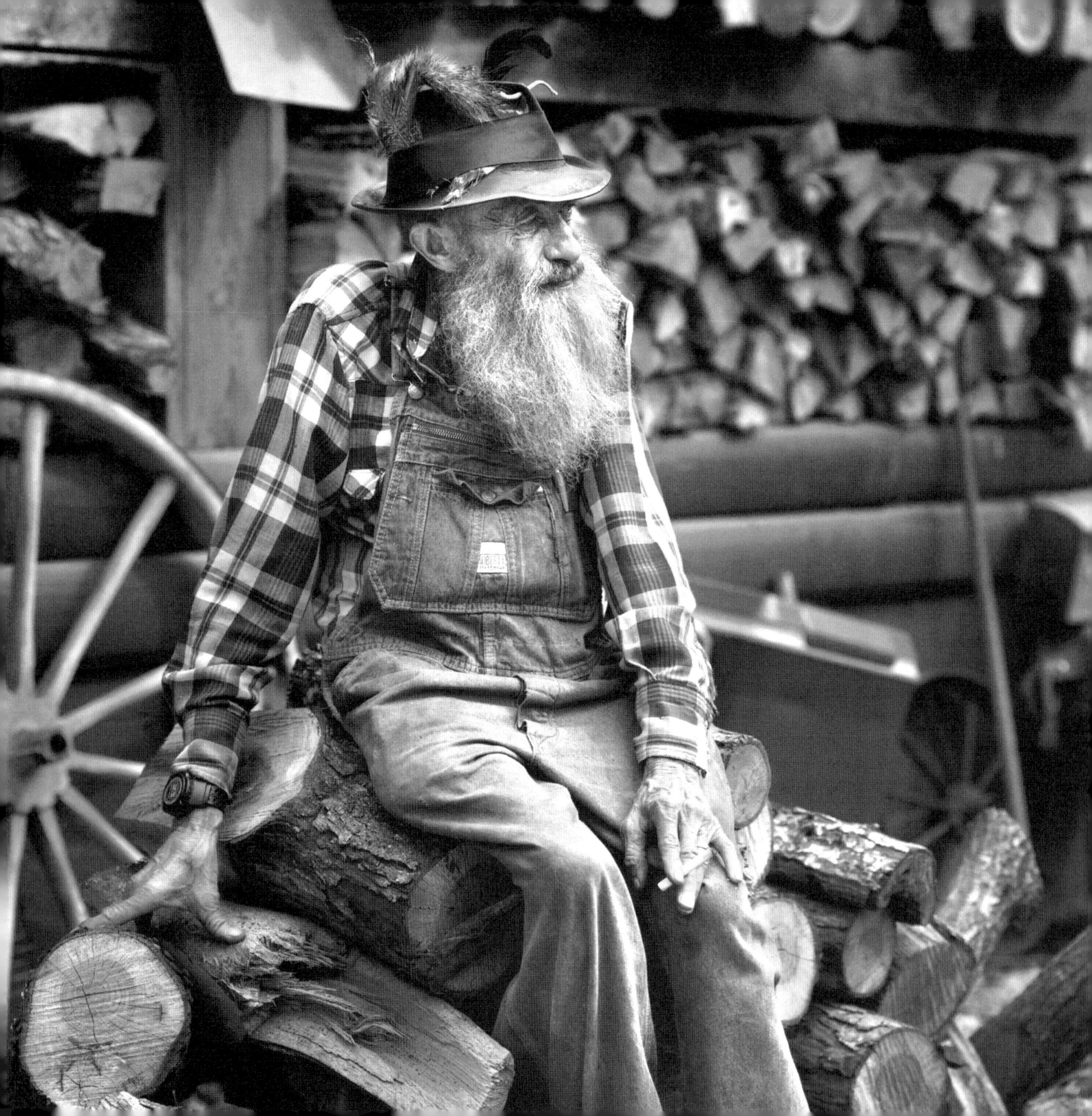

"Hell, I've sold likker to everybody in the world. I can't remember who I've sold it to and who I didn't. So he just kept on till he got the goods on me and they come down on me, all in one day."

-Popcorn Sutton

OUT OF JAIL and on probation, Popcorn got busted again by selling moonshine to a federal agent in a sting operation. This time, he was charged not only with moonshining but with possession of a firearm by a convicted felon. According to a newspaper account citing court records, Popcorn's previous convictions were for moonshining (with the usual probation), tax evasion and felony assault with a deadly weapon (he wasn't kidding about his big Case knife or the pistol he always carried).

What they found, according to the Knoxville paper, the News Sentinel, were "guns, three 1000-gallon stills, more than 800 gallons of moonshine and hundreds of gallons of sour mash and other ingredients."

The paper also reported that Popcorn had some of his moonshine in a shed and some in an old school bus that had been junked. ATF agents also found more of Popcorn's moonshine in a storage unit in Maggie Valley. Popcorn always said he made most of his moonshine "for export," meaning for sale there.

It's serious business for Popcorn this time around because with the added charge of firearm possession, it's a federal case to be tried in federal court, where they don't love

Popcorn like the local county courts do. Federal sentences can be longer, too, with more time served because there's no parole or time off for good behavior in federal prison. In the federal pen, the sentence is strictly "day-for-day."

In April, Popcorn pleaded guilty in federal court in Greenville and was allowed to spend time at home on monitored house arrest while he waited to be sentenced. When it came, the sentence was as stiff as one of Popcorn's 190-proof top shots: he was given two concurrent 18-month terms by U.S. District Judge Ronnie Greer and ordered to spend three years on supervised release once he got out. No probation this time, not even considering Popcorn's age and health. "This case didn't involve someone making moonshine in their back yard," the *Knoxville News Sentinel* quoted the judge as saying. "He was making hundreds of gallons at a time."

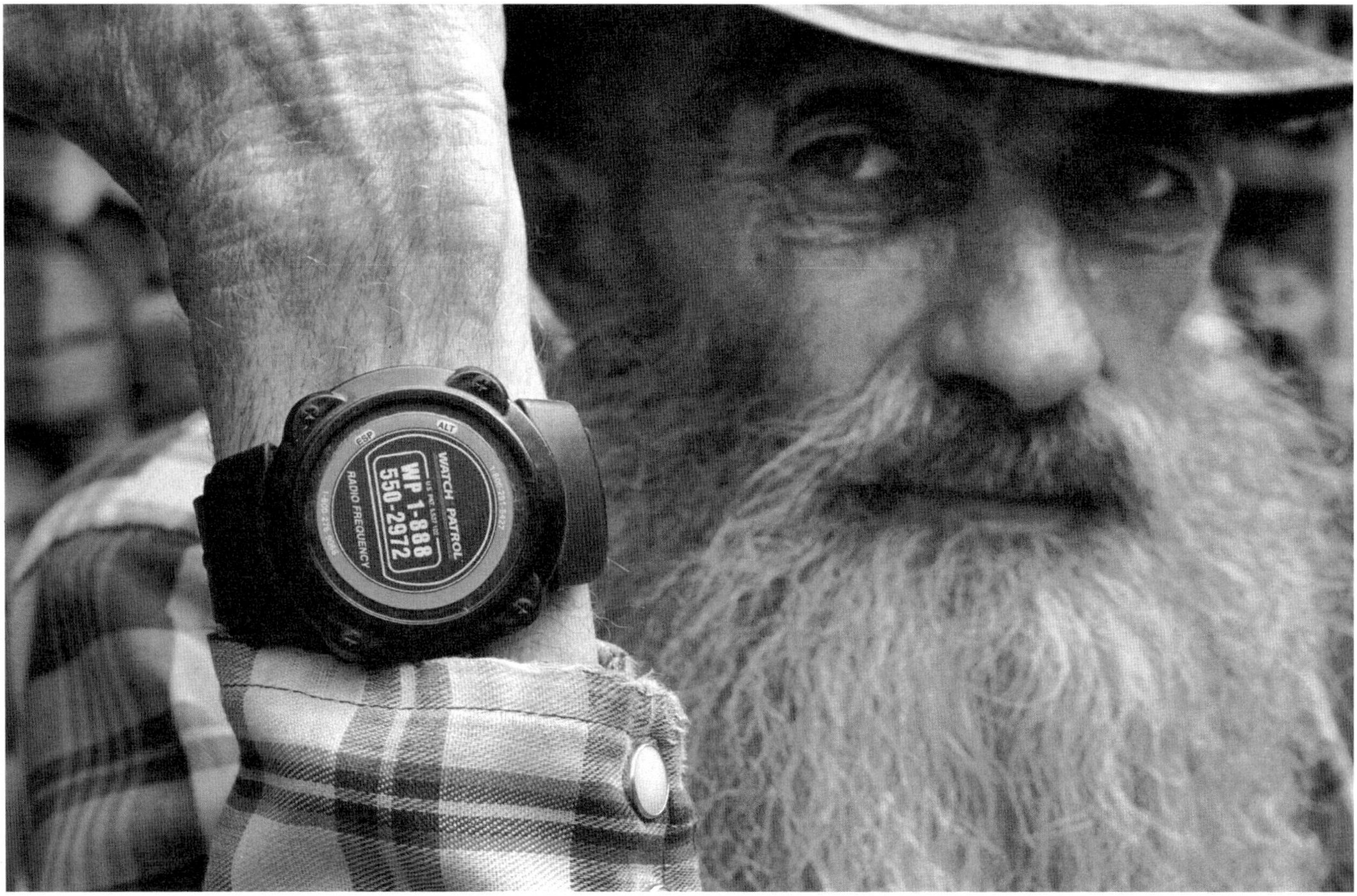

Popcorn's "Dog Collar" - GPS Tracking Bracelet

Don and I had one final interview and photo session with Popcorn at his home while he was awaiting sentencing. The house, now with Pam living there, looked about the same as it did the last time Don and I were there. The still house was gone, of course, burned to the ground by the fire. Anything left standing had been bulldozed. Nearby trees that had been scorched by the fire were the only evidence that Popcorn's stillhouse once stood there. The evidentiary trees were barely alive, but a few leaves were coming back.

Most everything metal had been melted. The stainless steel pots that were once used to cook beans at the Stokely plant had survived but were hauled off by the law for evidence since they "strongly suspected" that Popcorn was making moonshine with them. Popcorn later swore for the truth that they just punched an easily repairable hole in the big steel pots and returned them later.

The heavy cast iron body of the coffee bean grinder from the old A&P, bulletproof to the end, was there, but the aluminum top that once held Arabica beans and finally Popcorn's malt, had been vaporized. Popcorn gave it to me and, after letting the East Tennessee History Center use it for an exhibit in the *Vanishing Appalachi*a show, I added some rusty old garden tool parts to it and turned the thing into what might pass to the uninitiated as garden art. Now it looks like a giant mutant potato bug guarding my landscaping.

The exact spot where the still house once stood had been turned into a garden by Pam and Popcorn growing – what else? – corn.

Popcorn was under house arrest at the time when I interviewed him on his porch. He ate his lunch, consisting only of some applesauce on a plate, as he wore what he called a "dog collar" (a GPS monitor), provided by the law, to make sure he didn't leave his property. Frail and thin, Popcorn said he weighed only about 85 pounds. His legs were thin as the "coon peter" in his hat. He appeared to be a broken man, and didn't have any hope at all that he'd get out of this one. He probably knew then that he'd kill himself before letting the legendary moonshiner Popcorn Sutton die in prison like a sick old rat in a cage.

NO PRISON FOR POPCORN

No one who knew Popcorn well ever believed for a minute he'd ever go to prison -- one way or the other. He'd said as much many times. Popcorn's health was failing and he was getting frail, looking far older than he really was at 62. Popcorn had looked like an old man for a long time, an old man whose face could've been a topographic map of a hard Appalachian life. If you really wanted to get Popcorn cussing mad, all you had to do was ask him how old he was. "None of your damn business," he'd say before the real cussing started.

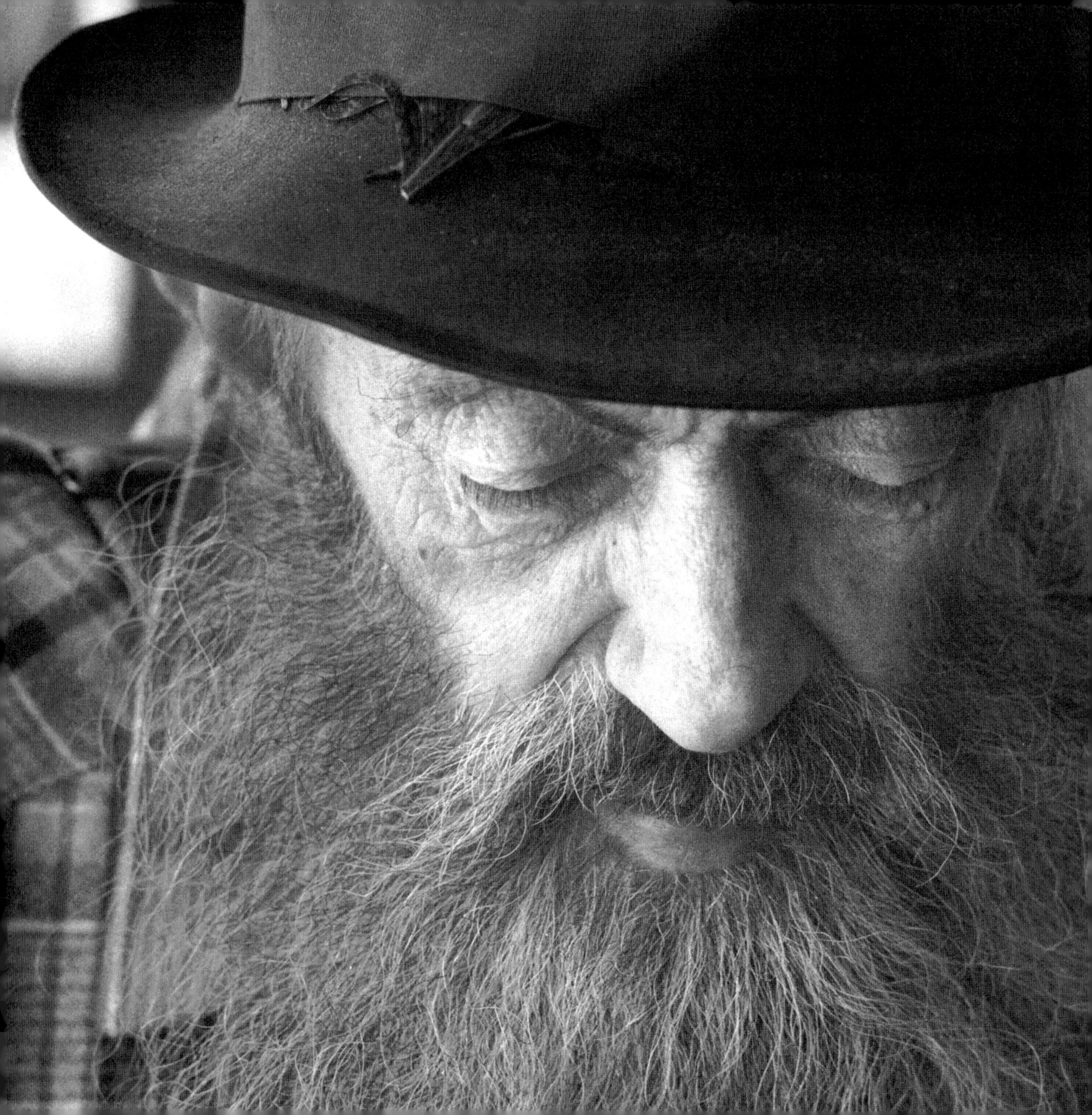

"Bible says 'judge not.' And I don't know yore heart for one bit for nothin' I just don't judge nobody. That's between them and the Lord."

Preacher Jimmy Morrow

WE BROUGHT WITH US that day Jimmy Morrow, a serpent-handling preacher at the Church of God in Jesus Christ's Name in nearby Edwina, another little community in Cocke County. Jimmy is a big man, but a big man gentle in both manner and spirit. Preacher Morrow practices his religion with a kindness every bit as powerful as the venom in the serpents he believes God has ordained him to handle without harm. He and Popcorn had both "growed up hard" in Cocke County as childhood friends and had remained friends for life.

While Jimmy contented himself with operating one of the porch rockers, I asked Popcorn to tell me what happened the day of the big bust.

"You mean when they got me March 13? Undercover guy got me, see. He'd made buys off of me before and he got me to where he's wantin' to buy me out, everything I had. I thought that was all right, you know. He's supposed to be a backer, said he'd knowed me for five years. Hell, I've sold likker to everybody in the world. I can't remember who I've sold it to and who I didn't. So he just kept on till he got the goods on me and they come down on me, all in one day.

"Them ATF people, man, it's just unreal what they'll do to ye. (ATF stands for the bureau of Alcohol, Tobacco and Firearms, a federal law enforcement agency that's part of the US Department of Justice that comes down on you if you're involved in "the illegal diversion of alcohol and tobacco products." They're also concerned with "illegal use and trafficking of firearms," among other federal crimes, so Popcorn qualified for a visit from them.)

"I mean, I can't understand it. They tore 'at house all to hell. They took all the money I had and put me in debt on top of it. I had to borry money to pay tax on that likker. They caught me with 1,600 gallon, you know, 800 gallon here and 800 gallon in North Ka-liner. If I'd a-had that I'd been a-settin' right."

When the ATF came to tear up Popcorn's house, they also took all the dollar bills he'd so neatly stapled to the ceiling of his small front bedroom.

How many agents came that day?

"Twenty-two. Got three stills. Big 'uns."

"Like the ones we saw?" I asked.

"Yeah. There's the top off one of 'em.," Popcorn said, pointing to a blackened stainless steel remnant in a trash burning pit he'd dug just off his front porch. "I had to have that much cut off 'fore it'd go in the buildin' I put it in."

Popcorn asks Jimmy if he's ever seen stills that big. Jimmy remembers hunting up on the ridges in his youth and coming up on lots of both silver cloud stills and copper pot stills, but none of either kind as big as Popcorn's stainless steel stills.

"Daddy said sickest he ever got was from drinkin' some of that ol' silver cloud stuff," the preacher said.

Jimmy continued, "I used to hear them moonshinin' stories from Uncle Lawson. I guess you knowed Uncle Lawson good, did'nche?"

"Yeah, he hepped me make a-many a run," Popcorn answered.

"Daddy drank a bunch of it, but I don't know if he ever made any or not," Jimmy said. "He drunk a lot of it, Daddy did."

There was a long silence. Popcorn turned to Jimmy and asked, "So what's your situation about drinkin', Jimmy? Lotta preachers'll put ye down fer it. What do you think about it?"

"Well, I'm a-lookin at you," Jimmy said.

"Look at me," Popcorn said.

So Jimmy continued looking at Popcorn and said, "Bible says 'judge not.' And I don't know yore heart for one bit for nothin' I just don't judge nobody. That's between them and the Lord."

Popcorn was quiet for a moment and I looked up from my recorder to see his eyes filling with tears before he finally spoke.

"He got it right, ain't he?"

The preacher continued, "I ain't gonna judge nobody. I don't know your heart. You been good people. You always been good to me. That's all that matters."

A cell phone rang just then from inside the bib of Popcorn's overalls. That gave Popcorn a merciful and well-timed exit from this emotional moment. Popcorn's cell phone also transported me from the 19th to the 21st Century with a brief stopover in the Seventies. The ring tone was the opening instrumental riff from the 1970 hit *Venus,* by Shocking Blue.

Popcorn pulled his cell phone from the bib of his overalls, where he always kept it turned on and ready. He looked at the caller ID and said, "That's my old neighbor. Calls ever day 'bout this time." Then, even though he knew exactly who was calling, he answered his cell phone in a crisp, businesslike way, saying the name he most loved to hear spoken.

"Popcorn Sutton."

I am Popcorn Sutton
from Maggie Valley
N.C. I have Made
likker all my Dam
Life That is all
I know how to do.
But I have Not Made
No Likker for a long
time I am Very
sick at this time

I have 3 Bleeding
Ulcers, Enfazema
Asthrites & High Blood
Pressure. I always
said I would Make
Dam likker till
I die, But I don't
guess I will get
My wish unless
A Miracle Happens

I have lived a rough
life But when Jesus
Cales me I am
ready to go.
Popcorn Sutton
Maggie V...

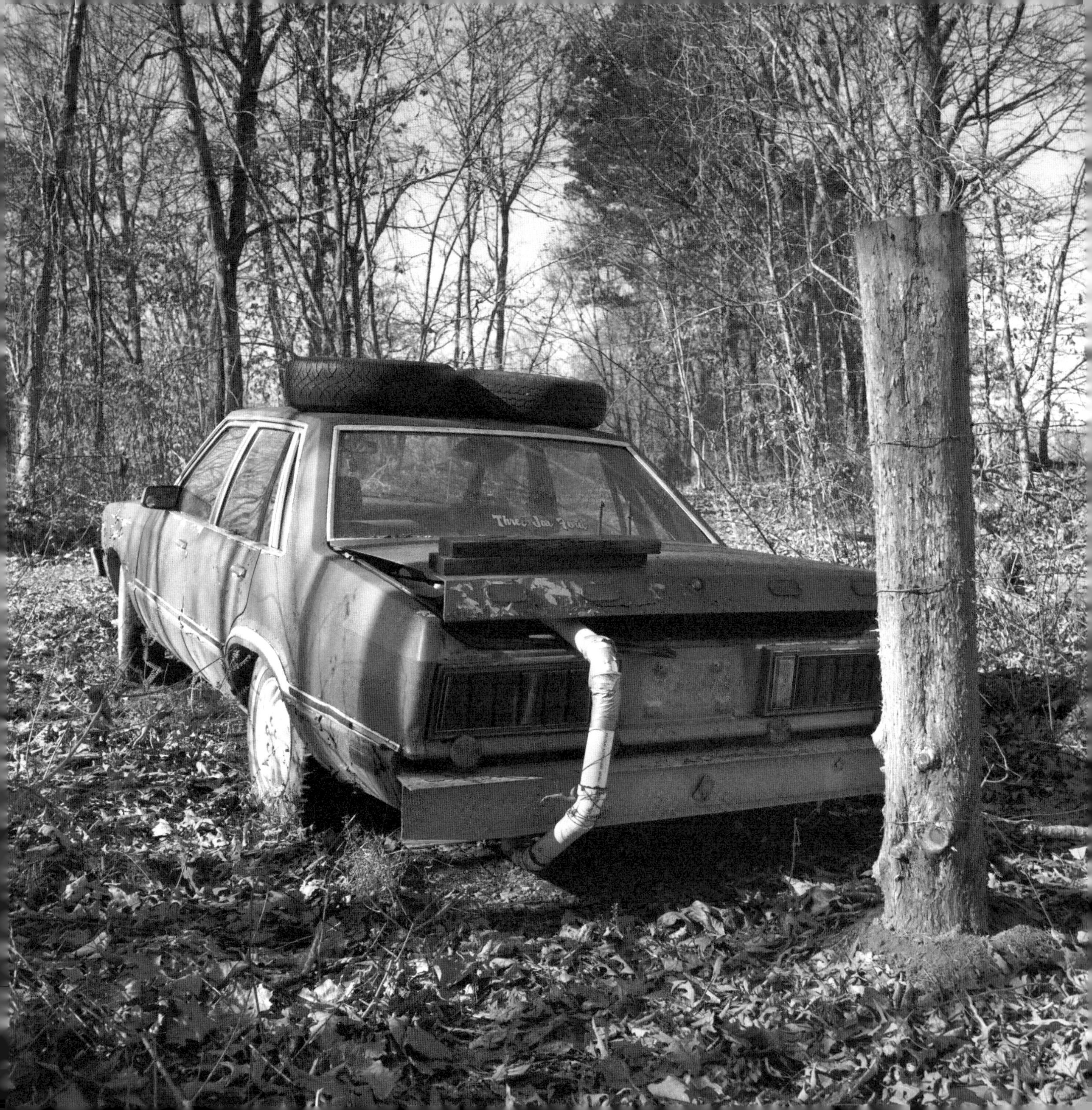

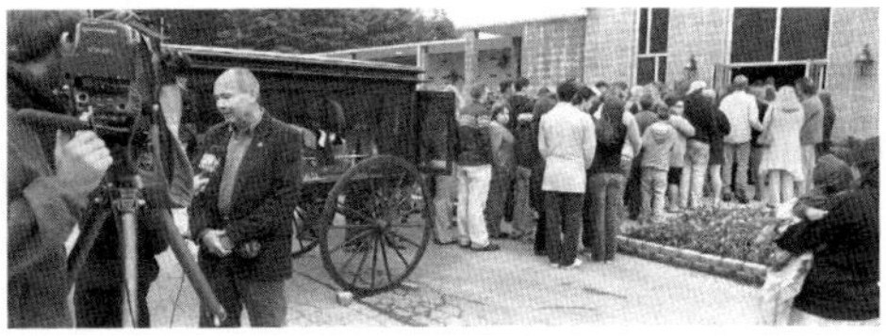

ON MARCH 16, 2009, three days before he was to be taken to prison to begin serving that sentence, Popcorn took his own life, beating the system again in his own way and on his own terms. He sent Pam out to do some errands and, while she was out, he made himself a little palette with some old blankets in the front seat of his "Three Jar Ford"— the same one I'd first seen in Maggie Valley. Then he rolled up the windows and started the engine so the carbon monoxide he'd channeled with PVC pipe from the exhaust up through the floorboard could do its work. Knowing the way Popcorn smoked, it's likely that he had one last cigarette, lit off the one before that. I can't say that for certain, but what I can say for certain, because Pam Sutton told me, is that the last message Popcorn left on her cell phone while she was out was, "I have always loved you and I always will."

Popcorn was buried the first time in Haywood County, N.C., where he was born, but there had been some damage to his tombstone (some say by vandalism, others say there was a family involved) so Pam decided to move Popcorn back to Cocke County, give him a celebrity memorial service and re-bury him at home where the still house was. That's where Popcorn is buried now, just a few yards away from the old "Three Jar Ford" suicide car which Pam has kept on the property.

Country star Hank Williams, Jr., showed up at the memorial service at the Rest Haven Memorial Gardens in Dandridge. He said he came because he admired Popcorn's philosophy of life, although he'd never met him. Later, it became clear as moonshine why Hank Jr. showed up at Popcorn's memorial service and was especially nice to Pam. He's since announced a business venture to make and sell a legal version of Popcorn moonshine - in partnership with Pam.

The mayor of Cocke County was there. He came because he was Popcorn's neighbor in Parrottsville. He and Hank Jr. joined hundreds of other people who came to fill the mausoleum at Rest Haven. After the service, Hank Jr. left to get on his plane and fly back home to Montana, but many who were already home stayed to join a procession following a funeral home hearse bearing Popcorn's body to Parrottsville. There Popcorn's casket with its Masonic emblem, the one he'd bought years ago at a bargain price and kept in his bedroom, was transferred to a 100-year-old black hearse driven by a retired Knoxville firefighter and pulled by two black Percheron draft horses.

The hearse made its way down the town's modest main thoroughfare, thence to a private and by-invitation-only ceremony at Popcorn's home.

Pam's cousin dug the grave with a backhoe, and there Popcorn rests today, with the custom footstone in place.

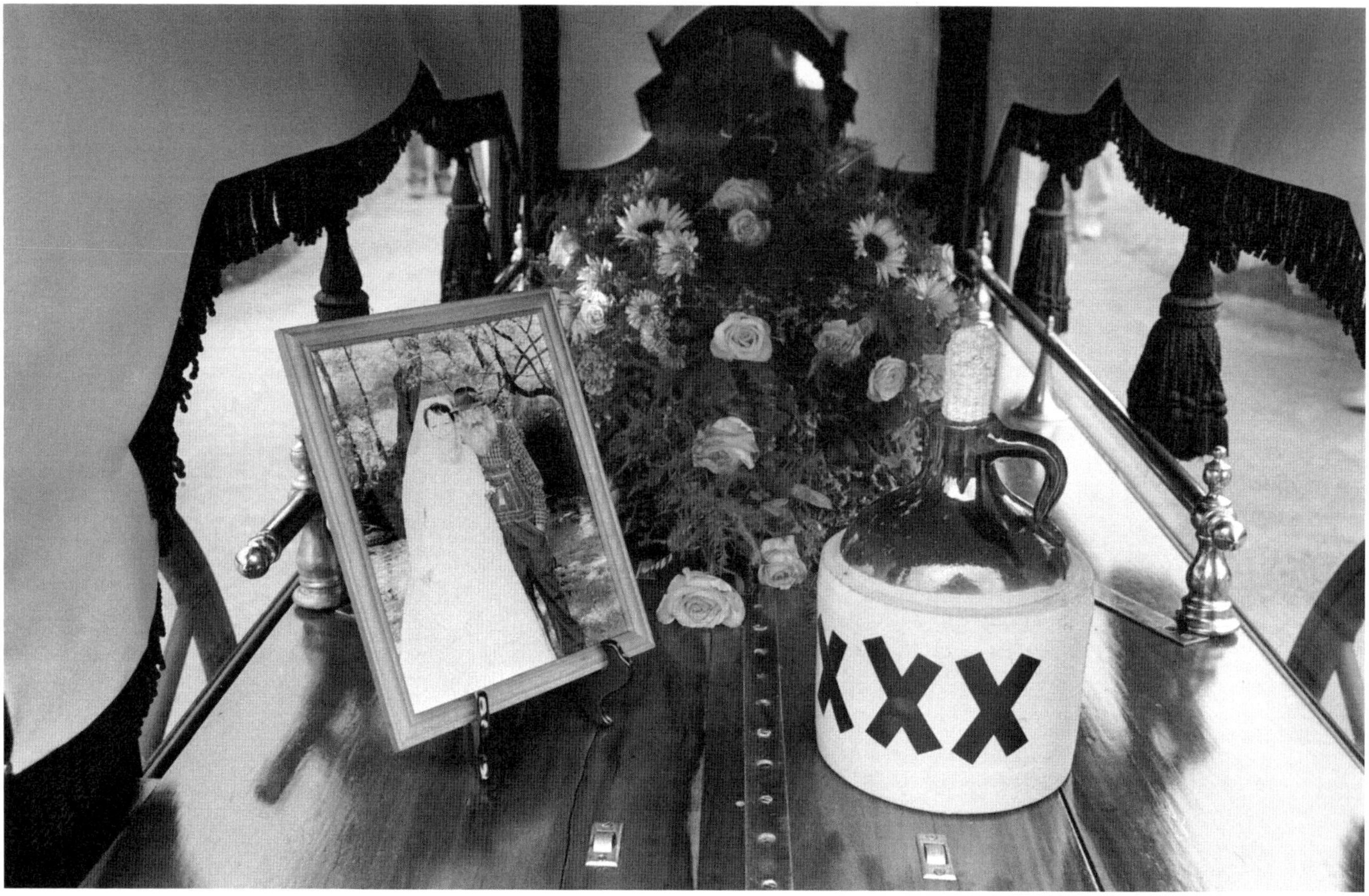

Remembrances of Popcorn at the Memorial Service

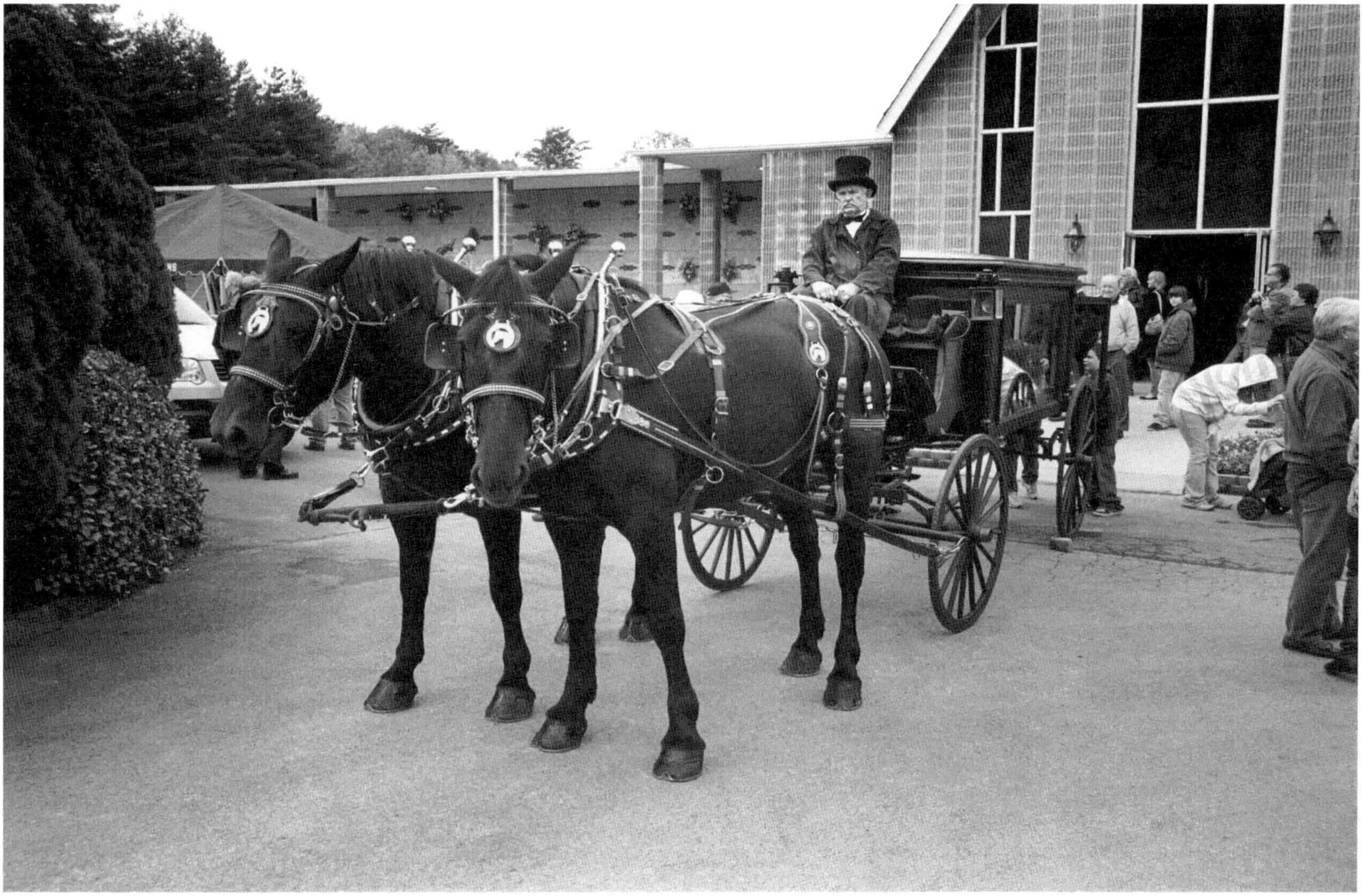

Horse Drawn Hearse at the Memorial Service

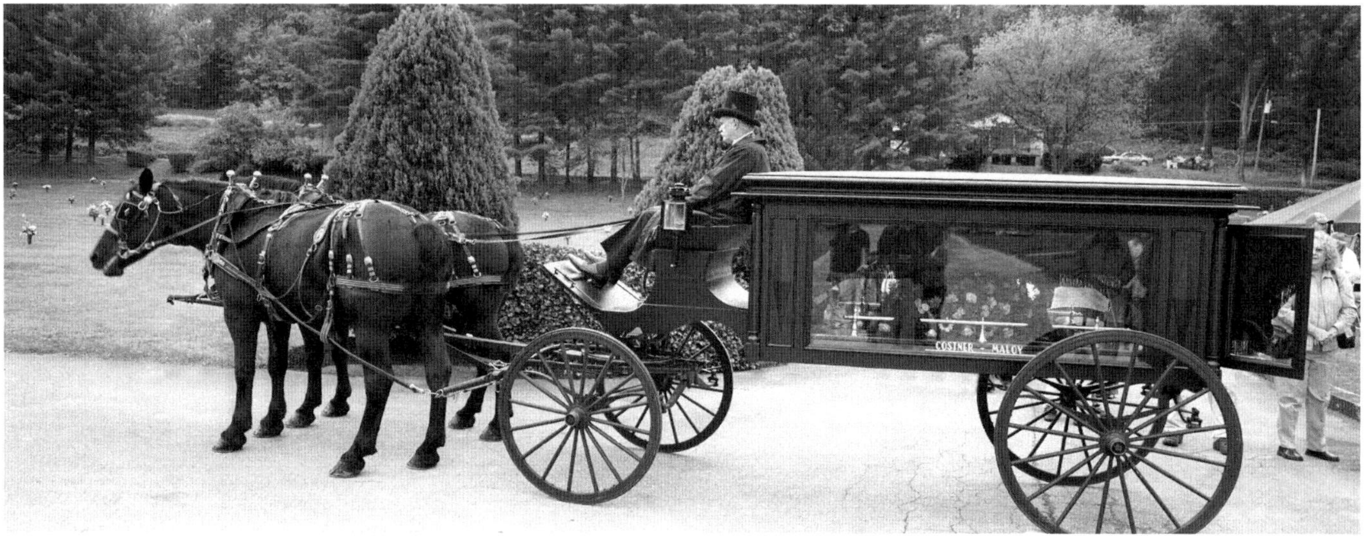

The Hearse

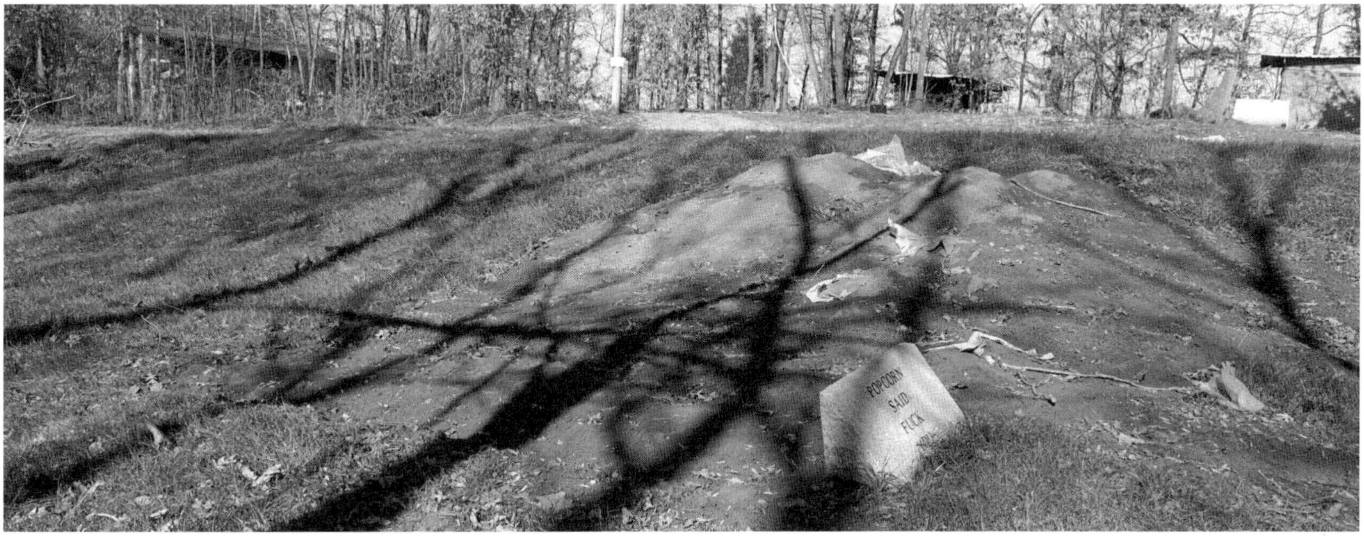

Popcorn's Burial Site Where the Stillhouse Once Stood

Corn and Sugar at
the same time.
then fill the Barrel
up to with in 8 in of
top of the Barrel
then after it ~~[illegible]~~ Cools
down ~~[illegible]~~ like Bath
Water add 2 Gal of
Corn, Rye & B[illegible]ley
Malt

Of Mash you Need[illegible]
Gal of Ground up Co[illegible]
Put the Corn an Su[illegible]
Both in the Barrel a[illegible]
the same time
then fill the Barre[illegible]
~~[illegible]~~ Half full of
Boiling Water
That will cook

[illegible]er it will start
[illegible] bubble in about
30 minutes then
By the next Morning
all the grain will come
to the top and it will
be working like Hell
when it Quits working
all the grain will
go back to the

[illegible]e Barr[illegible]
[illegible]eady
[illegible]r
[illegible]ind run
it The first run
which is Called
sweet Mash But
it won't Make But 2-3 Ga[illegible]
after you run it
Pour all of it Back
then it becomes sour

WE RETURNED TO Popcorn's house a few months after his death to talk to Pam and do another interview and photo session for the *Vanishing Appalachia* show. We wanted to find out how Pam was doing and what life was like after Popcorn.

At the time she was trying to eke out a living selling autographed copies of Popcorn's self-published book, *Me and My Likker*. Popcorn had left her with about 2,000 copies he'd painstakingly autographed for her, undoubtedly knowing that he was going to take his own life, leaving nothing behind. He had no money, since the law took it all. And, of course, Popcorn wouldn't be one to carry a lot of life insurance, other than a pistol.

Don thought that as a way to help Pam out, maybe this was a good time to tell her about Popcorn's secret stash of moonshine. Maybe she could sell it and make some money.

When Pam came to the *Vanishing Appalachia* show as an honored guest that following March, I asked her if she'd found the stored moonshine behind the false wall in Popcorn's old shack.

"Yeah I did," she told me, "And you know what? It'd all evaporated. Wad'n a drop of it left."

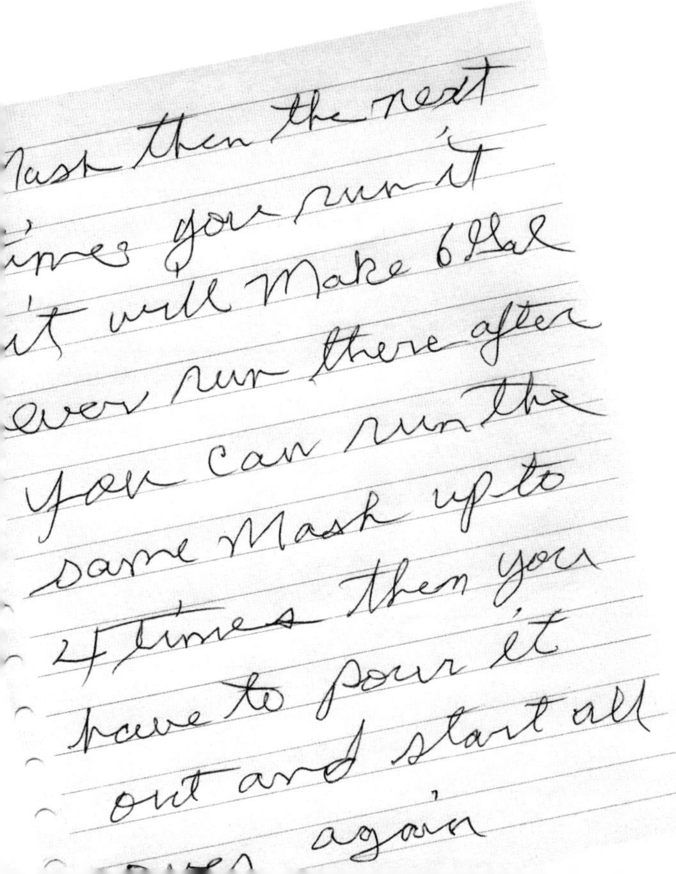
last then the next
times you run it
it will Make 6 Gal
ever run there after
you can run the
same Mash up to
4 times then you
have to pour it
out and start all
again

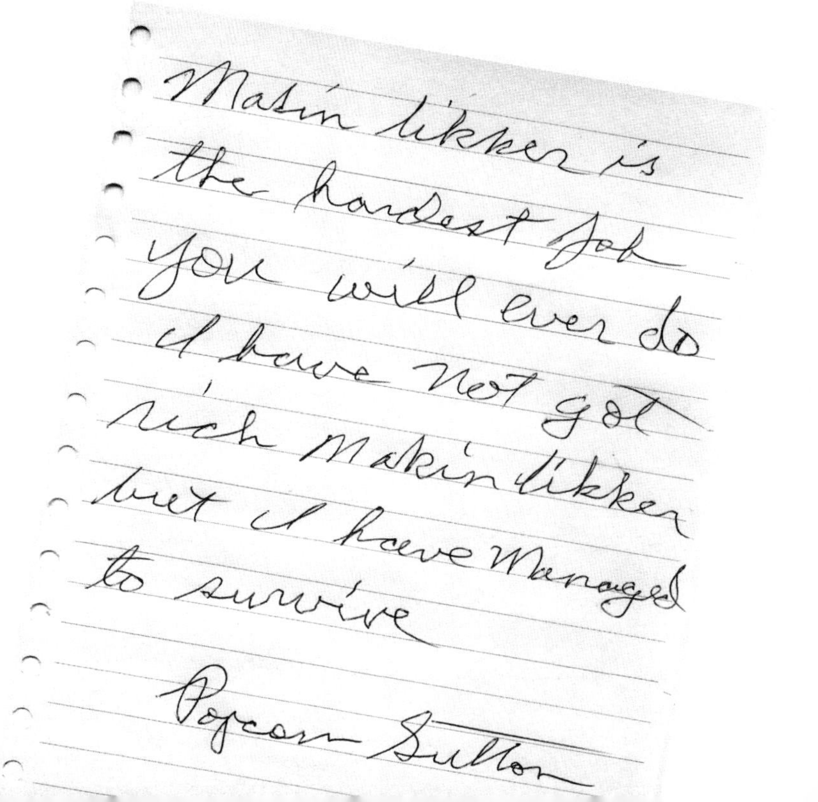
Makin likker is
the hardest Job
You will ever do
I have Not got
rich Makin likker
but I have Managed
to survive

Popcorn Sutton

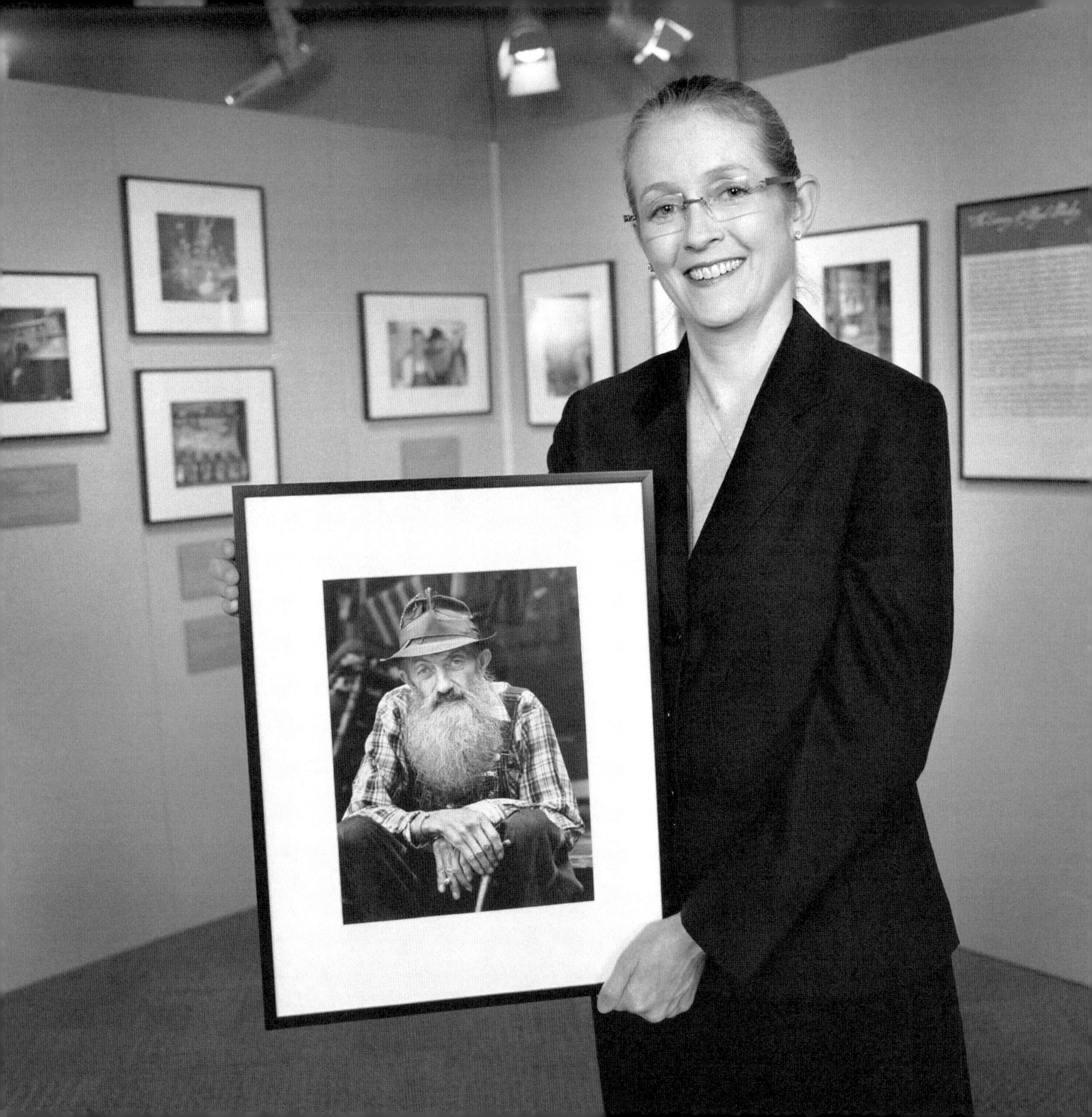

SINCE THEN, THERE'S been some more family feudin' over the rights to *Me and My Likker*. The legal dispute began when Regina Sutton Chennault showed up from Alaska bringing with her a birth certificate she said proved that she was Popcorn's only legitimate daughter and rightful heir. Regina claims she's discovered 12 people around the country fathered by Popcorn. She also asserts that Popcorn was married four times, but never divorced. So, following her claim to be Popcorn's only legitimate heir, she's filed a federal lawsuit against Pam, not only for rights to the book, but also the right to visit Popcorn's grave "and say the Lord's prayer." She's now a devout Roman Catholic.

She's also a nationally-known trauma surgeon in Anchorage, Ak.

The story of how she went from being a moonshiner's daughter living in a trailer in Parrottsville to being a trauma surgeon in Alaska is as long as the drive from East Tennessee to Alaska. One of the most fascinating parts of her narrative is that she says her interest in trauma surgery began on a Sunday afternoon she remembers vividly from her childhood. She was six years old. She was in the trailer with Popcorn, watching TV while a group of men drank moonshine outside. She heard an unsteady but persistent thudding on the front door and opened it to see a man standing there with a knife stuck in his neck.

"I don't know whatever happened to him," Regina says, "but I do know that from that moment on, I became fascinated with what was inside the human body." Before that she says she wanted to be a mechanic but thought she probably was too small to work on cars. The only other thing she dreamed about was having new clothes to wear and enough to eat. When Popcorn left Regina's mother, an aunt took her to Houston, Texas, where she did finally get new clothes and enough to eat and started making straight A's – enough to get her a full college scholarship to Rice University. Her grades in undergraduate pre-med were good enough to win her another full scholarship, this one to the University of Texas Medical School at Houston.

There, she met the nationally known trauma surgeon Dr. Red Duke, best known outside of Texas for a syndicated television segment that ran for years (The Doctor Red Duke Show), and for being the emergency room doctor who attended Texas Governor John Connally, who was wounded during the Kennedy assassination. Dr. Duke mentored newly-minted Dr. Regina S. Chennault and helped her get the job as a trauma surgeon in Alaska.

It's been a long road indeed from the living room in Popcorn's trailer to the emergency room in Anchorage, but that's the way Popcorn stories and Popcorn-related stories go.

Popcorn's book was first published in 1999 and re-issued after his death.

It's sold well since his death at $50 a copy -- at least the autographed copies, anyway. I have an autographed copy myself I bought from Pam. The book is tough to read, the same way Popcorn was sometimes tough to listen to. But the book, like the man who signed it, is an irreplaceable piece of Appalachian history and I thought worth the price.

Since his death, Popcorn's fame has been magnified into something he would be very happy to brag about, inveterate publicity seeker that he was, but that fame has also intensified the family squabbling over rights to his book. Regina's claims will probably be settled only when her lawsuit is heard in court. Everything about this matter is complicated, so it won't be easy.

In the meantime, Regina says she's been tracking down children sired by Popcorn now living in various places around the country. One of them, Sky Sutton, of Northampton, Mass., has also written a book about Popcorn called *Daddy Moonshine*. Sky's been quoted as saying she's estranged from her father and hasn't seen him since she was two years old. Popcorn's current family says Sky Sutton's a liar and they hate her.

Well, there's no feudin' like family feudin' in the mountains. At this writing, the suit over rights to Popcorn's book hasn't been resolved, but so far at least nobody's been shot, so there's that.

THE LAWSUIT

REGINA'S SUIT claims legal rights to Popcorn's book because she says he wrote it on his own, and since the book was really his, it should be hers now. One point she makes is that Popcorn did have some help writing the book from Ernestine Upchurch, who's since assigned whatever rights she had to Regina. Ernestine Upchurch was not credited in the revised edition Popcorn finished in 2008, but there's a forward in the book written about Popcorn from the point of view of someone who knew him well. It's clearly not written by Popcorn himself. The last paragraph of the book's forward reads:

> When Popcorn realized that very few people were willing to put in the hard work necessary to build a good "pot" or to make good liquor, he wanted to pass on his experiences with the trade. He tells a humorous story, many of his anecdotes have been changed to protect his friends and true events are told on those who have died. He decided to write "Me and my Likker". Read with pleasure and understanding. His flow of language is sometimes colorful and obscene. It is the way he expresses himself. He is real.

There's a space for a byline at the end, but there is no byline; it's obviously been removed in this edition.

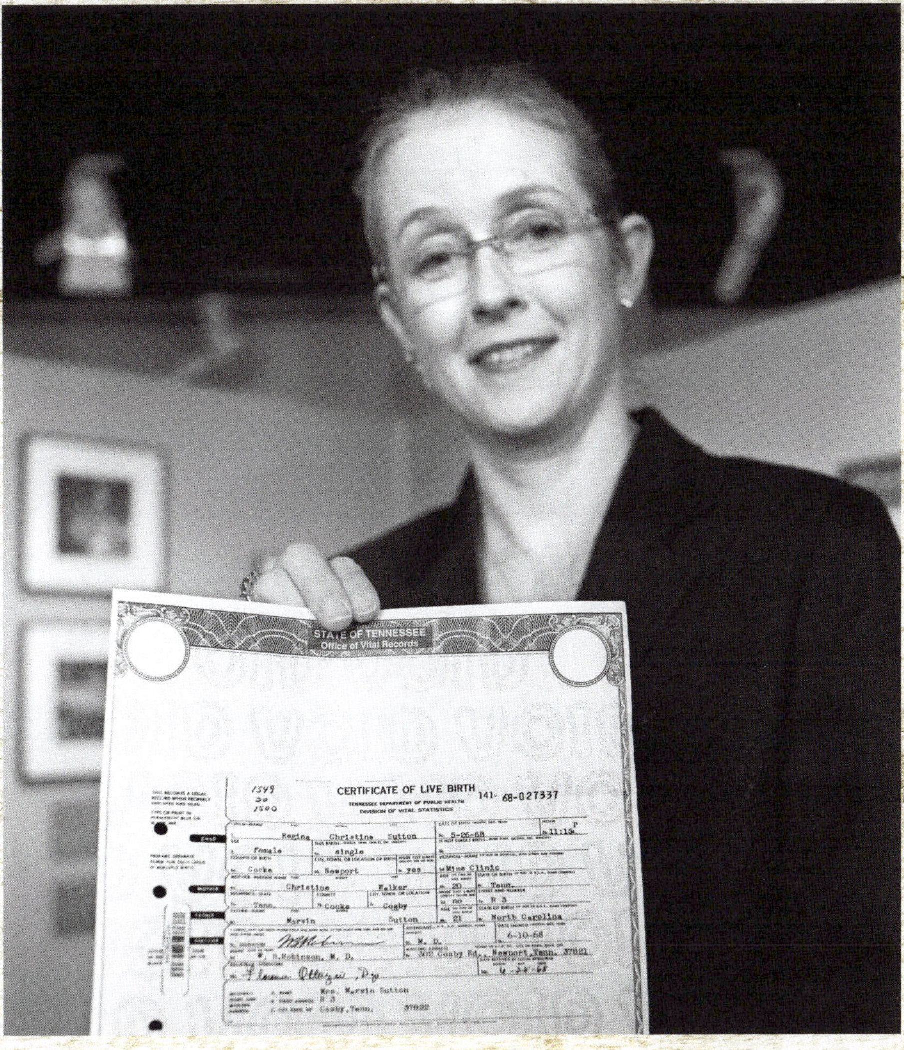

Popcorn lived with Ernestine at that cabin on her property in Maggie Valley back in the 1990s and their relationship did not end on good terms, so that explains the missing byline. Regina says this is partly why Ernestine Upchurch assigned her copyright to Regina Chennault.

In her answering affidavit, Pam said Ernestine Upchurch isn't mentioned in either the original or revised edition as co-author, and insists that neither Ernestine (who isn't a party to the suit) nor Regina has rights to any royalties the book might produce.

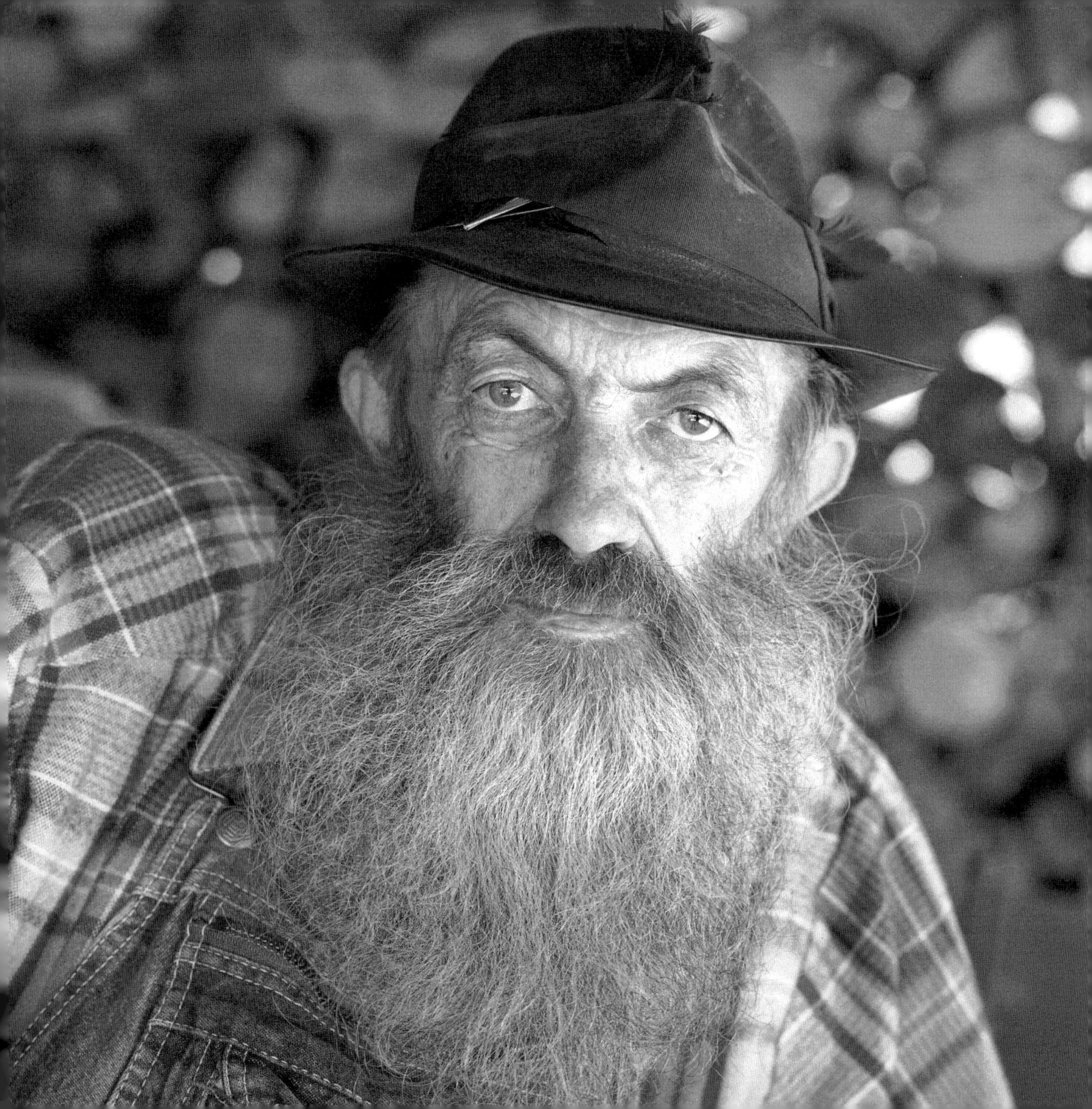

THINKING ABOUT POPCORN, who he was and what he represented, I concluded that Don had been right all along in what he thought about Popcorn when he first met him. Yes, Popcorn was the embodiment of a colorful stereotype, and he knew how to work it. But behind that, behind all the outlaw bragging and the down-to-business marketing, Popcorn was absolutely the real thing, a genuine Appalachian mountain man moonshiner.

He became a folk hero because he refused to abide by the rules set out by the aristocracy who have always preferred the lower classes under their rule make a living with honest toil, doing work they approved of. And do it with gratitude, without so much as a whimper of complaint.

Like the authority-hating hardscrabble Appalachian culture he embodied, Popcorn also had a softer side. He could be warm, charitable, generous, loyal and, as Pam Sutton will tell you to this day, a romantic fool for love.

Whatever else he was, keep in mind that Popcorn was also a career criminal in the sometimes nasty and violent business of moonshining. Simply put, moonshining can kill people and cause people to be killed. It should never be overly romanticized.

It also has to be said that when Popcorn died, something iconic and real from old Appalachia died, too. But unlike the last evaporated drop of Popcorn's secret stash of moonshine, his legend, and the Appalachian mountain culture that sustained it, won't go away so easily.

Moonshine, meanwhile, made and marketed legally under several brand names, has been enjoying a trendy popularity around the country, probably thanks in part to Popcorn and his notoriety. This could've made Popcorn rich legally. But you can be sure Popcorn would be having none of it.

There ain't no such of a thing as a legal moonshiner, Popcorn would say, and he was a moonshiner to the end.

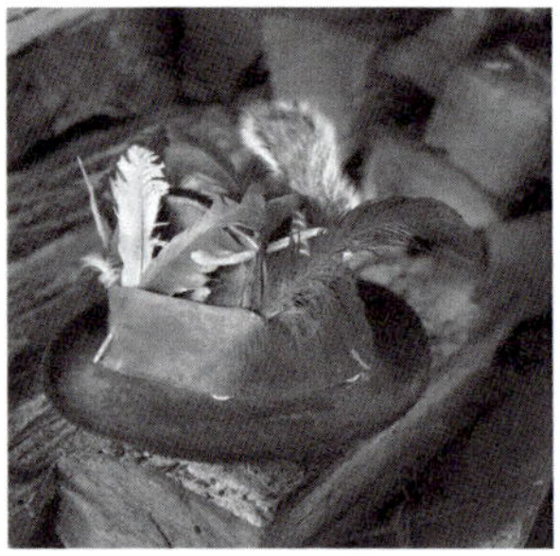

"I have lived a rough life
but when Jesus calls me
I am ready to go."

-Popcorn Sutton

41560186R00042

Made in the USA
Lexington, KY
18 May 2015